T0326074

"*After Atlantis* contains the down to earth secre
masters. They have distilled the principles needed
lems through participation. Save yourself ten years: read *After Atlantis.*"
—**Gifford and Libba Pinchot**, authors,
Intrapreneuring and *The Intelligent Organization*

"*After Atlantis* provides a practical road map to separate the quick-fix
traps from the more long term organizational and work improvement
approaches to get us through these turbulent business times."
—**Dennis Tachiki**, Sakura Institute of Research,
Center for Pacific Business Studies, Sakura Bank, Tokyo

"I found *After Atlantis* to be a thoughtful and pragmatic peering into the
future. I recommend it to those who plan to manage in the 21st century."
—**Philip Crosby**, Chairman and CEO,
Philip Crosby Associates II, Inc.

"As a research manager I sometimes feel like I have motion sickness—and
they want me to hit ever-moving targets! *After Atlantis* tells managers how
to deal with the challenge of creating and sustaining adaptive organizations. Anyone not wishing to feel like a seasick captain in the coming
decades should read this excellent piece of work."
—**S. E. de Bie,** Research Director, Department Public-Private Sector,
The Court of Audits, The Netherlands

"A practical guide for setting up a new corporate culture and involving
everybody in the company."
—**Theo Dilissen**, Adjunct Director,
ISS Europe, Belgium

"This book is not simply a toolbox of random ideas but rather contains
the cornerstone pieces for a lasting structure. The international author-
ship points to the fact that the challenges described are more common
than many suppose—and that solutions are based on humanity, not
nationalism."
—**Pat Townsend**, coauthor,
Commit to Quality and *Quality in Action*

"An extremely user friendly, concise, and practical text that presents a set of guiding principles and procedures that can be adapted to a wide variety of organizational settings and cultures. I have been unable to put it down (I've even reread it to make sure I didn't miss anything!)."
—**J.M. Blackbourn, Ph.D.**, The University of Mississippi, School of Education, Research and Training Center for the Handicapped

"This is the first book in a decade that gives a practical non-cookbook framework of how to excel in the whitewater environment of the 21st century. A must read for those who hope to enter the next millennium more self-assured and optimistically."
—**Charles Ehin, Ph.D.**, Professor of Management and former Dean, Gore School of Business, Westminster College of Salt Lake City

"*After Atlantis* offers us a rare opportunity, should we be disposed, to recapture an age when all things ran well. All it takes is an open mind and the will to persevere."
—**Dick Danjin**, International Representative, UAW

"Simply stated, hard hitting, and challenging. How refreshing to hear someone cite the importance of learning with a little humor thrown in to remind us not to take ourselves too seriously in such a serious world."
—**Jackson C. Bundy**, Executive Vice President (retired), The Greenwood Area Chamber of Commerce, South Carolina

"If you despair in your soul about your future, or the future of your organization or community, read *After Atlantis*. Then you will understand that we are all talented and so are you. The authors help you to learn in precise and practical ways how to activate these talents in yourself, in others, in your organization, and in your community."
—**Freek A. M. ten Herkel**, Managing Director, Van Ede & Partners, Career Management, The Hague, The Netherlands

"Ned Hamson has once again proven himself a linchpin in the organizational improvement movement by bringing together a group of excellent minds to help us rediscover our direction and to show us how to get where we want to go."
—**William Roth, Ph.D.**, author, *The Evolution of Management Theory* and *A Systems Approach to Quality Improvement*

"Change, innovation, and lifelong learning are the key words for modern society. And this is what you will find in *After Atlantis*—how to put ideas into practice. In it you'll be given the tools of making your business successful, environment-friendly, and future-manageable. Very live and entertaining reading. It will surely find its reader in Russia—a smart and creative individual who cares about being able to successfully work and adapt to the changing world of the 21st century!"
—**Dr. Julia Sorocoumova, Ph.D.**, Senior Researcher, Russian Center for Comparative Education, Russian Academy of Education, Moscow, Russia

"A must reading that takes its place in the first rank of books on innovation and change. The authors have caught the essence of the universality of working, leading, and managing in turbulent times. The processes and methods presented create a practical, comprehensive, and inspiring guide for creating a new golden age in an organization, a community, a nation, and even in one's self."
—**Gloria Martillano**, co-founder, Tuloy Sibol Foundation, Manila, Philippines

"Give someone a management course and they'll manage for a day. Give them *After Atlantis* and they'll manage for a lifetime. It's a practical, thought provoking book on leadership for today and tomorrow. Excellent!"
—**Robert Specht**, Manager of Corporate Training and Recruitment, Telephonics Inc., Farmingdale, NY

"Fascinating reading and right on target for today's leaders. The focus of *After Atlantis* brings home the critical communication skills of leadership—not speaking and writing, rather listening and understanding."
—**Dr. Bobby Papasan**, educator and former Superintendent, Tunica, Mississippi Schools

"The authors have contributed to the changing of cultural conditions necessary if we are to develop the kind of thinking and productivity tomorrow is demanding."

—**Dr. Dennis Rader**, educator and author, *The Jasper Problem: Rethinking Reductionism and Developing an Ecology of Education*

"I spend most of my time developing the system, process, and settings that enable people to take a high road of getting together, getting along, and doing what we need to do. I see *After Atlantis* as helping leaders do that job better."

—**Fire Chief Allan Brunacini**, Phoenix Fire Department, Phoenix, Arizona

After Atlantis

After Atlantis

Working, Managing, and Leading in Turbulent Times

Ned Hamson
with
Frank Heckman
Tom Lyons
Kaat Exterbille
and
Peter E. Beerten

Routledge
Taylor & Francis Group

LONDON AND NEW YORK

First published by Butterworth-Heinemann

This edition published 2011 by Routledge
2 Park Square, Milton Park, Abingdon, Oxon OX14 4RN
711 Third Avenue, New York, NY 10017, USA

Routledge is an imprint of the Taylor & Francis Group, an informa business

Copyright © 1998 by Taylor & Francis

All rights reserved.

No part of this publication may be reproduced, stored in a retrieval system, or transmitted in any form or by any means, electronic, mechanical, photocopying, recording, or otherwise, without the prior written permission of the publisher.

Library of Congress Cataloging-in-Publication Data
Hamson, Ned, 1944–
    After Atlantis : working, managing, and leading in turbulent times
/ Ned Hamson with Frank Heckman ... [et al.].
        p.   cm.
    Includes bibliographical references.

    1. Management.   2. Crisis management   I. Title.
HD30.19.H35   1998
658—dc21   97-22330
                                                                    CIP

British Library Cataloguing-in-Publication Data
A catalogue record for this book is available from the British Library.

ISBN - 978 0 7506 9884 9

Dedication

I'd like to dedicate this book, on behalf of my colleagues and myself, to the mythical worker *Hans N. Feet*. Hans always wanted to bring his brains and spirit to work with him, but was told to leave them at the plant gate—all that was wanted were his hands and feet. Today's and tomorrow's workplace needs the whole person. So this if for you Hans.

I would also like to dedicate this book to the readers' grandchildren and great grandchildren—I hope in using it, you can create workplaces free of fear and filled with people who can find as much meaning and joy in their work as they do in their lives outside of work.

Ned Hamson

Table of Contents

Preface

Working, managing, and leading in turbulent times . . . Chaos and opportunity are the twin choices for individuals and organizations as one era ends and the shape of the one to come is as yet unknown. Many of us are tempted to look back at the past era or age with more than a little regret that it is no more. The past is inviting because, in hindsight, the rules are known and we know what to expect. I suppose that's why it is said that the military is always planning for the last war (oftentimes with disastrous results). The past is inviting also because we humans, like all living things, have a basic need for predictability—predictability enhances species survival. During past transitions between ages or eras, it seems that this looking back either did little harm or may have even been a healthy part of searching for the rules of a new future. Today, however, we have a new problem. As a not-so-ancient sage, Yogi Bera, might have said: "Even the past ain't what it used to be."

The golden age, the Atlanean Age, for individuals, institutions, organizations, and cultures, used to be a time of giants, those who launched great advances or who wrote their ideas and lives so large that they were the pattern for the ages to follow. A *back to the basics* movement would be a time to look at the essence of what made an age golden. But today, with so much more information available about the past than before, who knows what or whose past to look back to?

So which past do you prefer? The 1940s? People lived and worked with purpose and a spirit of sacrifice during the war years. Millions also died. The 1950s? A rebuilding time for most and a boom time for the U.S. Colonialism had not quite lost its grip and full civil rights were not yet available to African-Americans. The 1960s? The fact that America's boom was an illusion being based on everyone else's rebuilding was not yet apparent. Great advances for the American, Japanese, and European middle class are co-mingled with little wars that grew larger and drained our spirits, with a false dawn of a yet to come era of love and freedom, with the bloody end-point of a decades long striving for non-white civil rights in the U.S.

You see the problem, don't you? We know too much about previous ages to glorify them without judgement. Yet we still could use some help in learning how to survive this transition and perhaps to become a leader in the age awaiting. You and I are not the only ones asking: "Well, if there really is no easily discernible golden age to look back to for inspiration, where do I look for help?" We put this book together to answer that question and questions like it.

The future, as we can perceive it now:

- Will not be dominated by a few players
- Will have few patterns that can be used for any kind of linear planning
- Will have more players and options than ever before

So how can we help you to survive and even thrive in this kind of turbulence?

1. *We clearly identify some of the major drivers of change/turbulence.* Knowing these drivers will help you to identify which of the many moving targets you should concentrate on. They can also serve as a checklist with which you can take the measure of the turbulence at any given time.

2. *We will share in detail some of the means for survival and thriving that have been carefully researched and field tested and are already serving a number of firms quite well.* Practical applications of flow or optimal experience research, open systems theory, the search conference, and participative design can and have become the keystone that holds what have been disparate or parallel improvement and involvement processes together into a coherent and adaptable strategically focused system.

The Shared Learning process (which can contain the search conference, participative design, and Total Quality Management [TQM] within it) is a robust and adaptable change design which can serve a single organization, as well as it can serve multiple sites within one organization, multiple organizations, or even a whole nation or segment of a nation.

3. *We examine the merits of discontinuous change and how an innovation cycle of your own making can be a guide and impetus to inventing your own future.* Applications of research on flow, open systems theory, the drivers of change, and Shared Learning are integral parts of operationalizing and creating your own innovation cycle.

4. *We present a concise and practice-based process to build communications planning and implementation into both your change process and ongoing operations.* The oil needed, or to use an information age term, the

bandwidth needed to ease the working of all of these methods/ approaches is a planned and thoughtful communication process. Most grand designs for change founder on a reef consisting of: "We said we wanted to do . . . but you're not doing it—didn't you hear us?" and "I said it once, isn't that enough?"

5. *We present an architecture with which you can understand how to launch and sustain a quality management/continuous improvement process.* Managing quality and continuous improvement have proved to be daunting tasks for too many organizations. There is a logic of where, when, and how to start. There is also a sequence to its planning and implementation.

With an understanding of all of these approaches, we believe that you will finally begin to see (as we have seen in practice) how you can create your own future. No magic bullets. No one or secret right way. What we offer here is loaves and fishes.

Loaves of bread represent for many the staff of life—that which sustains us and our organizations. What we offer here are the basics to making good bread, your own bread, the way you and your customers like it. Why does this analogy work? If there was one right and best bread, everyone would already know its ingredients and know how to cook it. But to accommodate both individual and changing tastes with the same ingredients and a wide variety of other additives we can make hundreds of different types of bread: bread, donuts, cakes, pretzels, scones, and pies. So for some of you, this is a book about becoming a master organizational baker and not a recipe book.

We are all familiar with the fish story: Give someone a fish and they'll not go hungry for a day, teach someone how to fish and they'll not go hungry in their lifetime. Our approach here is similar but takes things a few steps farther so you will be ready to begin a journey to becoming a master fisher. To carry this analogy a bit farther, we will help you understand the function of bait, lures, nets, and poles as well as how to make your own; how to spot conditions for good or poor fishing; how to find different ways to get to your fishing hole, as well as how to overcome barriers to getting there; and finally, the secret to making sure that the community (organization) thrives and never hungers again, involving everyone in learning how to become master fishers. So for some of you, this is a book about a master organizational fisher.

We are not trying to be corny or simplistic with these two analogies. We are only saying what you already know:

- "There is no one off-the-shelf way to sustain my organization in the times ahead."
- "I need a way to integrate all the different approaches we have been using or are thinking about using."

We believe that we have brought together for you a number of approaches and methodologies that are not only compatible but synergistic with each other. With these, we believe you and your colleagues can create and nurture a sustainable future for your company, your agency, your customers, or your community.

. . . NED HAMSON

Editor's Acknowledgments

Many helped me get to this point of being able to share this treasure house with you. There are too many people to just write down a list (it would be a very long list). My heartfelt thanks to colleagues Frank Heckman, Tom Lyons, Kaat Exterbille, and Peter E. Beerten. They each hold vital parts of the successful organization of today and the future. In working together, we hope we have modeled a good portion of what this book contains. These same heartfelt thanks to the other contributors to this book: Steve Barber, Merrelyn Emery, Robert Holder, and John Guaspari. Each of them provided essential pieces to the puzzle. My thanks also to the Association for Quality and Participation and its thousands of present and past members. They have both inspired and sustained me. And to two of the best volunteer proofreaders: Frieda Hughes and Nancy Stamper. Thank you, thank you, thank you.

Atlantis: The Song

"The continent of Atlantis was an island which lay before the great flood in the area we now call the Atlantic Ocean.

So great an area of land, that from her western shores those beautiful sailors journeyed to the South and the North Americas with ease, in their ships with painted sails.

To the East Africa was a neighbor, across a short strait of sea miles.

The great Egyptian age is but a remnant of The Atlantean culture.

The antediluvian kings colonized the world.

All the Gods who play in the mythological dramas.

In all legends from all lands were from fair Atlantis.

Knowing her fate, Atlantis sent out ships to all corners of the Earth.

On board were the Twelve:

The poet, the physician, the farmer, the scientist, the magician, and the other so-called Gods of our legends . . ."

—DONOVAN

Printed with permission of Donovan (Music) Ltd. London, England, copyright 1968.

Part 1

After Atlantis

Chapter 1

Working, Managing, and Leading in Turbulent Times

*Ned Hamson, Association for
Quality and Participation*

S tories of the wonders of Atlantis, the turbulence which preceded and followed its destruction, and the yearning for its resurrection abound. For many, such a story represents a fabled golden age of what might have been, or what could be again, if only we were wiser or stronger.

The reasons given for the fall and destruction of the Atlantean Golden Age range from timeless greed and internal dissension to arrogant disregard for the impact of their power to violent forces of nature from which even their mighty powers could not save them.

Each of us is familiar with or has been touched by a personal Atlantis that flowered and fell with such sudden force that all seemed chaos afterward. We recognize or know people who, left in its seemingly patternless wake, cling to the hope that their Atlantis will rise again, or who seek to create a new Atlantis which ritualistically pays homage to the Golden Age.

The most recent Atlantean age for the U.S. took place during the 1950s and 1960s. The yearning for a return of that golden age or the desire to recreate it can be found in frustration driven remarks from all levels of society, business, and government. Remarks such as these are still quite commonly heard:

> "In the 50s and 60s we dominated the market and introduced new models every year! We should be able to do the same today!"[1]

> "We put a man on the moon and now we don't seem to be able to even put bread on the table or a roof over everyone's head!"

Similar remarks can be heard in nearly every organization that had a period of rapid growth or when they were the respected leader in their field. Statements like "I remember when we . . .," or "Why can't people work together like we did when . . ." are recalling some organizational golden age. Good memories and inspiration from past accomplishments are worthwhile and are instructive. However, when these memories are a substitute for understanding forces at play in the present and in the foreseeable future, they leave people and organizations open to being whipped about by the turbulence which follows the end of any golden age.

Here are some examples of what the American Atlantis looked like:

- Cincinnati, Ohio was a world center for the milling machine industry.
- The mighty American steel industry stretched from Allentown, Pennsylvania to Gary, Indiana and Chicago, Illinois, and then south to Birmingham, Alabama.
- The Big Three automakers (GM, Ford, and Chrysler) ruled the world auto market.
- Elgin, Gruen, Bulova, and Timex timepieces kept time for the world.
- Xerox created a new industry, revolutionized office work, and wiped out the need for carbon paper.
- IBM electric typewriters and mainframe computers created a second office revolution.
- Kodak was photography from camera to finished film.
- Television, radio, record players, and tape recorders were GE, RCA, Zenith, Magnavox, and Sylvania.
- Broadcasting was ABC, NBC, and CBS.

---

[1] These golden years were in large part based on:

1. Meeting the pent up demand of American consumers during the Second World War.
2. A boom in the number of children under age six.
3. The need to rebuild war torn Europe and Asia.
4. The demand for the next four decades, for military and aerospace products in response to the challenges of the Cold War.

This list could go on and on. For each of these industries, organizations, and for American culture, as a whole, the 1950s and 1960s were indeed a golden age, a time when for two decades, they served as the world's new Atlantis. But the American Atlantis has fallen. Those who deny it or try to recreate it with old approaches will not succeed. They too will fall. It matters not whether you are in the private or public sector. The golden age of stability and competition between just two, three, or four competitors has ended! We are now in an age of turbulence, of white water, of apparent chaos.

WHAT DO I MEAN BY THE WORD TURBULENCE?

What does this turbulence look like? Here a just a few examples of the waves, whirlpools, and rip tides of the last few years:

- Hypertext Markup Language (HTML) and the World Wide Web (WWW) have changed the nature of the Internet in less than one year. In cyberspace, a company of one or two people can look just as impressive to the world as the giants can. The notion that a large amount of money is necessary to attract customers or to get your message out has been disproved in less than 12 months.
- There were three major auto producers in the U.S. in 1958. By 1980 the U.S. market was divided up between GM, Ford, Chrysler, Nissan, Toyota, and Volkswagen. Honda carved out a significant share of the American market in three or four years. Mitsubishi, Infiniti, and Hyundai created shares for themselves in less than two years.
- As the telephone, Internet, and cable/satellite television converge, numerous companies, markets, and technologies will be destroyed and reinvented in the next two to five years.

Let's assume for the moment that I have said all the right things and you are now convinced that we have entered an age of turbulence. A world in which new players can enter and carve out a significant share in your market in less than two years. A world in which the market-creating and market-destroying power of a Xerox plain paper copier or a desktop computer could appear from any corner of the globe.

Your first question might be, "If the old solutions and questions no longer apply, what are the correct approaches and questions?" My reply would be this:

- The correct question today is not, "How do I recreate the conditions under which we thrived in the past?"
- The correct question is not, "How can I control my environment and bend it so that we can be a fixed and prosperous island where once a continent stood?"

- The correct question, or at least a good starting point is to ask, "What are the primary forces at work in today's turbulent environment and what types of approaches might I use to create success for myself, my organization, my community, or my nation?"

Good, I am glad you asked that question, because that's what this book is all about.

1. We are going to name and describe some of the primary drivers of change in both the private and public marketplace, as well as the drivers of change within workplaces.

2. I will outline some workable countermeasures based upon practical approaches developed in the field. Each countermeasure will have an article to refer to for more information in the back of the book.

3. I will suggest a way that we might think about an overall approach to change and innovation. With several methodologies, our hope is that people will be able to create their own path or bridge to make their own way through the turbulent waters.

4. My co-authors will then, each in turn, discuss at length a major component of this overall perspective or approach.

Our goal is that when you have finished reading the book, you will have a better idea of what you need to think about, work on, and implement to give you, your employees, and your organization a good shot at success for the next several decades.

THE DRIVERS OF CONTINUOUS CHANGE AND TURBULENCE

Someone said, "It would be easy to hit the target every time if it would just stop moving." In the past that might have been a line in a story or joke about someone who drinks too much alcohol. Today, sadly for some—gladly for others—it could easily be a remark at a marketing meeting or a rueful comment from one software engineer to another.

Why the Targets Keep Moving

The targets keep moving because there are dynamics or patterns of individual and group psycho-biological behaviors which are always in motion, developing new or more complex patterns which are then played out in technology and society. Said a little more simply, change is driven by the playing out of patterns of individual and group emotions, interests, and biological needs. Said even more simply, change is driven by the interplay of human beings' two sets of needs: biological and psychological.

Biologically, humans need predictability and control to assure its survival as a species. Anything that endangers our ability to reproduce ourselves is a threat to the species. Psychologically, humans need change, novelty, and meaning beyond our biological selves. They need to create things which please us, as well as things that make working and living easier. There is no solution or balancing point to this dynamic. It creates a very basic tension which as one pulls in one direction, the other pulls in another direction. It is a dynamic that you will recognize in some of the other dynamics which I will present shortly.

Patterns, Dynamics, Tension, and Fractals

Playing out a basic dynamic or tension is what others might describe as a fractal in human behavior—a pattern that as it is played out and repeated over and over again creates larger and more complex structures. Each of these drivers might also be thought of as fractals that after being set in motion, create ever-changing and larger structures or systems.

The principal difference between these fractals and those that might produce a whirlpool or a crystal, is that human fractals think and are self-aware. The variation they produce is therefore much greater than simpler, more predictable fractals. The other point to make here is that the context or environment that the fractal finds itself in has an impact on how it plays itself out.

But, lets get on with it. It's much easier to see these things as we talk about them in real terms.

1. ALL WORKERS, FROM THE BOARDROOM TO THE FACTORY OR OFFICE FLOOR WANT GREATER INPUT INTO THEIR WORKLIFE AND WORK PROCESSES

This is the employee involvement, teams, empowerment, self-managing team trend. It is the result of a deep desire to express and apply democratic ideals in every aspect of our lives and society. Can you think of any institution or structure in our society where our beliefs in democracy are not trying to express themselves? I think not. All aspects of society are touched by it. It's not democracy with a big D and it doesn't mean that people want to vote on all company decisions. A friend who works with many different types of organizations puts it this way: "Even old-style bosses don't want to work for old-style bosses any more." Keep in mind that as an organization's context or environment changes, people will interpret the need for involvement in new ways. Even customers and stockholders now want a role, or a greater role in organizations.

Struggle against this trend at your peril. It will not weaken nor go away. Ed Lawler's latest research indicates that high involvement leads to healthier bottomline performance.

2. LOW COST AND HIGH QUALITY ARE NO LONGER SEPARATE CHOICES

Consumers know that they can expect and demand both low cost and high quality. These twin low cost and high quality expectations are working their way, sometimes together and other times separately, through American society and its organizations in a steady manner.

The low-cost/high-quality expectation is permanent. Only a general world-wide depression could change this. People have experienced or seen in product after product, service after service, that cost goes down and quality improves. They will no longer accept shoddy goods or service (even in government) for long from anyone.

3. THE "WHAT'S NEW?" FACTOR

Let's turn to another long-term factor or dynamic that drives change throughout the world: the irrepressible urge for all things new and shiny. In the U.S. two people who have not seen each other for a week or so approach each other on the street. One says, "What's new?" The other says, "Nothing much." The first person may think or even say "Oh, that's too bad."

The "What's new" question is so common in the U.S. that few of us are aware how much it colors our worklives and lives as consumers. It is a characteristic that's both a blessing and a curse.

The "What's new" question is good because it drives people to tinker and improve things. It's bad when it pressures people to think that something they do or have is deficient because it's not brand new.

I think the negative aspect of "What's new?" comes from the expectation that social or organizational innovation should mirror the pace of technological innovation. The value attached to technological innovation is that new is always better, or at least desirable. The negative aspect is that often gimmicks are used to make something look new (thus having added value) or to rename something so it appears new.

Quality Circles, Tiger Teams, and Team Management

I recall a conversation with a quality circle facilitator some years ago that went like this: "Ned, my manager (who never paid much attention to our quality circles) just read an article about team management at NUMMI and now he's all hot for us to stop doing quality circles and to do NUMMI or team management. What's the difference between them?"

"Not much," I replied. "If you add some cross-functional circles, some management circles, and some task circles, you've done it. Just tell him they're pretty much the same thing."

My friend replied, "He won't buy that. He's been told that team management is the new thing and he always wants to do the new thing."

I thought a moment and then said, "Well, why don't you tell him that Tiger teams and Wolf packs are even newer than team management and that's what you want to do. Then tell your circles to continue as before but with a name change to Tiger teams (caution them not to tell anyone else that they're doing the same stuff). Then tell the managers that you're going to introduce the Wolf pack concept to them so they can address strategic and cross-functional problems. Then take your training manuals and change the words 'quality circle' to 'Tiger team' in one version and to 'Wolf pack' in another version." Don said, "Seems silly, but it will probably work." It did.

What's New? Toyota and Datsun Gain Footholds in California

During the mid to late 1960s, Toyota and Nissan (then Datsun) gained a foothold that has since expanded their reach across North America by offering something new. No, I am not talking about their legendary obsession with quality. The new entry point for them was to offer an automatic transmission, an AM/FM radio and whitewall tires (remember them?) in the base price of the car! This was a big deal to California car buyers. Not only were the cars and trucks cheaper and got decent gas mileage, but we could get the standard add-ons as part of the package! Who says all innovation has to be technological? More about this later.

The point is that through offering something new that the then Big Three automakers didn't and wouldn't, Datsun and Toyota got a foothold on buyer loyalty. When they (along with other Asian automakers) later added outstanding quality, they were on their way to a 20% plus share of the North American market. In making a smooth way to advance their future, the Japanese automakers created turbulence for everyone else.

4. I WANT IT MY WAY!

Newness is not the only driver of the market or management approaches. Many consumers and employees are not only feeling and saying, "I want new, I want quality at low cost, I want more control over my job and life." They are also saying "I want all this and I want it my way!"

From fast food to cars, bicycles, clothing, and jobs, people want the convenience, cost, and quality of mass production and in just the way they want it—customized just for them! Have you stood on line at a local MacDonald's and seen 5 out of 6 people ordering their Big Macs with five different specifications like I have? Their food system is designed for mass production of prespecified units and their customers now want it all slightly customized to their taste at the same price, speed, and quality!

So the challenge is either to figure out how to mass produce high-quality, low-cost customized products and services or to become a niche or specialty firm. It's a challenge that few organizations are meeting. But those who are, will win the day.

But the old high volume producers are still successful, aren't they? Yes, the IBMs and General Motors still seem to be hanging in there. The question is, "How much longer will they survive if they don't figure out how to respond to the challenge?" If you look at the *Fortune 500* or the *Forbes 500* in decade slices, you see that every 20 years or so some really big producers fall off the list or go away entirely. Who would have thought that PanAm would have disappeared so quickly or Eastern Airlines?

MANAGING INNOVATION

We are just now getting an inkling of how to manage innovation and create and sustain organizations which are highly adaptive to their environments. The ideas of Hidaki Yoshihara in a 1990 issue of *The Journal for Quality and Participation* point one way to approach innovation:

> **Respected innovation versus disdained innovation—**
> Unconventionality or differentiation can be divided into two types. The first type gains the respect of competitors and other companies: "Ah! What they are doing is very good. It's beautiful." The second is the type of differentiation I have been talking about today from the beginning: the "It's absurd" differentiation. This type of differentiation invites other companies, including competitors, to scorn and make fun. There are many instances in which the "It's absurd" differentiation, which is scorned by other companies, is more effective than the differentiation that gains respect. Is this due to chance? No, I don't think so. Disdained differentiation is better than respected differentiation, why? There are two reasons. The first

reason is that other companies are slow to imitate "absurd" ideas. "Ah! What they are doing is very good. Let's do it, too." This is the kind of reaction prompted by the type of differentiation that wins other companies' respect.

In a fiercely competitive market such as Japan, respected new products such as Minolta's A7000 camera, or Funai Denki's home bakery equipment are imitated almost immediately by other companies and a tough competition starts. The originator of the idea does not even have time to obtain the entrepreneurial profits.

On the other hand, there will be no immediate imitation in the case of "absurd" strategies, since other companies tend to think "That's ridiculous!" "Poor guys . . ." Only later, when success becomes quite obvious, the attitude changes to "It seems that they were right, let's try it anyway." Thus, the company can enjoy the promoter's profits and, sometimes, can build a strong position in the market.

CREATING ADAPTIVE ORGANIZATIONS

Another approach is one developed by Fred and Merrelyn Emery of Australia and their colleagues in the U.S. and other parts of the world. They have spent the last 25 to 30 years refining and simplifying the socio-technical systems analysis approach first developed at the Tavistock Institute during the 1950s and 1960s in the United Kingdom and later in Norway. They and their colleagues have written eight articles in *The Journal for Quality and Participation* over the past two years that describe their practical and effective search conference methodology for strategic planning and participative design methodology for redesigning work processes. Motorola, Hewlett-Packard, Microsoft, and Xerox are just four companies who are using these approaches to great advantage. You will hear of many more in the next few years.

When the approaches of Yoshihara and the Emerys are married together with an employee-involvement oriented approach to Dr. Deming's thoughts on concept of variation, a firm has a good chance of meeting the challenges just discussed.

THE TOTAL OR COMPLETE TRANSACTION

I should add one more perspective to the stew before leaving this section. John Guaspari wrote an article a few years ago that stressed considering the entire transaction between you and your customer and not just whether they are satisfied with the product or service delivered. In other words, the customer is judging, you, your company, and its products and services from the time he or she hears about it until the product or service is delivered and used—you have many chances to satisfy or dissatisfy the customer. I would go a bit farther and say that you are being judged during every active or even passive interaction between yourself and the customer. The Toyota and Nissan example illustrated that newness need not be in technology.

Your challenge is to consider where and how to introduce customer-pleasing innovation in the entire transaction between the two of you. The larger challenge is how to build innovation into all of your processes so that you can meet the "I want it now, with high quality, low price, new, and made just for me!" customer. The successful manager and leaders of the 21st century will have figured out how to integrate innovation into their systems.

THE INNOVATION CYCLE

We really need to think in terms of at least a four phase cycle of innovation or improvement:

- Discontinuous innovation
- Continuous improvement
- Breakthrough improvement
- Another discontinuous innovation

Discontinuous Innovation

Discontinuous improvement or innovation is the type that Yoshihara referred to—the type that reinvents a market, product, or significant aspect of the customer transaction. Another way of thinking about it is as a market destroying product or service or a product or service which disrupts the environment for your competitors in what was formerly a highly competitive market.

Continuous Improvement

This is the type of improvement or innovation that is normally addressed in Total Quality Management (TQM) or total quality control work-teams—individuals and task teams that look for ways to continuously improve their processes or to align work process in a manner which improves productivity, service and/or quality.

Breakthrough Innovation/Improvements

Breakthrough improvements can be characterized as those that greatly enhance an existing product or service by making it less costly, easier to use, or better looking. When Shewart and Deming talked about not tinkering with processes that were in control, they also noted that the only way to get improvement at that point was to redesign the process. The successful organization in turbulent times will be one that manages all three types of innovation and then returns to the beginning of the cycle so they will have a constant stream of products to serve all of their customers.

If you adopt this view and manage for the innovation cycle, what would it look like? It might look like this: Your breakthrough innovation is your next candidate for killing off or selling off. Eh? But that's crazy, isn't it? Not really. You can kill it off, sell it off, or license it because you are just introducing your new product or service that makes your old new and improved one obsolete to your customers.

5. THE JUST DO IT! OR LET'S PLAN IT! WHIRLPOOL

When I was flying from the U.S. to Australia a few years ago, I had this vision of two compelling cultural statements that differentiate U.S. and Japanese cultures.

- Just do it!
  The first is the Nike slogan "Just do it!" If there is any phrase that resonates with or captures our image of the American spirit, it is a *Just do it* attitude. It drives creativity and innovation, and is what makes the U.S. one of the most entrepreneurial nations on earth (at least within its startup sector). This is its positive side. On the negative side, it also drives the short-term view which many decry.
- Let's plan it!
  Let's plan it! Our two main competitor groupings, Japan (along with Hong Kong, Singapore, South Korea, and Taiwan) and Germany are consummate planners and even seem to enjoy it! It drives their obsession for engineering in both quality and reliability as well as the ability to get high-quality, mass-produced products to the market very quickly. Their planning capability is their strength and is one that the proponents of TQM maintain the U.S. must adopt whole heartedly if it is to catch up.

Yes, planning in great detail is a virtue and a positive response in turbulent times. It also has its downside. Some over zealous TQM folks maintain that we have to plan and improve everything in excruciating detail or we'll fail. Let's think about that for a moment. How long will it take in a typical American organization (or in your own thinking) for the *Let's plan it* approach to bump up against the core of creativity—*Just do it!*—and you find yourself saying, "Let's get on with it, I've got a job to do!"

Balancing Just Do It and Let's Plan It

Don't shake your head and give up just yet, Robert Schaffer in two articles in *The Journal for Quality and Participation* gave us a glimmer of how to transform these apparent opposites and to create a reasonable balance that will support the positive thrust of just doing it and planning it.

When talking about how to introduce total quality or continuous improvement to an organization, Schaffer recommends asking those from the top to the bottom the following question:

> What problem or what process needs improvement right now to keep your heads above water in the coming year?

It never takes long for Schaffer to find a consensus around that problem or process. If you follow his lead, you have the place to begin your improvement process.

Next he suggests training the people as they go to work on the problem so the training will provide immediate and positive results. This is his excellent way of balancing just doing it and planning it. You combine high motivation to get it right and to do so in time to save your company or job.

A variation of this approach is to ask people in your organization an additional question:

> What opportunity do you see that we'd be absolute fools not to try to take advantage of in the coming year?

When people answer both of these questions, you will know the areas where *Just Do It!* and *Let's Plan It!* will work together, rather than oppose each other. It will give you a good start on creating a strategic breakthrough for your organization. It is also the environment or zone within which quality and participation will flower best.

When you have successfully solved a big problem or taken advantage of a big opportunity, people may well get the idea that they can apply the same approach to their unit or to their own job. Further success at that level will give people the experience and confidence to keep applying quality and participation methods to more and more areas, while not burying the spirit of their *Just do it!* strength.

6. IS IT USER FRIENDLY?

Oh? You thought this was old hat and one that you could ignore? No way. The customer still wants products and services that are user friendly. Why? Because very few of us really want to solve puzzling manuals, dials, or automated telephone gateways to get to use the product or service we need. The one solid rule that everyone should never, never, never forget is this: If you make the product or service easier to use or access, customers will select your product or service over another if . . .

Of course there's an if. The product or service still has to be high-quality/low-priced, available now, and customizable if at all possible. For those who want an example or two, here they are:

- Most folks will choose the VCR that they can program easily over the one that only their five-year-old can work. This is especially important in homes with no five-year-olds present.
- If Apple Computer Company hadn't priced their products so high, the choice between a Macintosh and any other PC would never have been a contest. No mail on this one please—I know there are people who actually like having to complete six steps before they can begin using a piece of new software. But in our office, before Macintoshes, only two or three people could and would use the PC clone. Within minutes, as soon as we got our first Mac, people were using them. Mac blew it on price and easy availability but they were and are still right on the money when it comes to user friendliness.

7. IS IT EARTH FRIENDLY?

This is no longer just a nice feature. As we come to better understand systems and ecology, we are quickly learning that we can't stand outside of nature nor its systems. The choices aren't really about saving jobs or saving cute but not economically important owls, plants, or fish. The fact is that the extinction of some living organism may well be a symptom analogous to a fever or a rash in a human system.

More and more customers are choosing to be more safe than sorry and to err on the side of caution. Companies that pay attention to those customers, will be rewarded. Those who take the next step, actively looking at the whole systems within which they operate, will be rewarded in both the medium and long run because they will find ways to do things which reduce the amount which is now spent on waste products or clean-ups. They will also be the inventors of the products and services most highly desired in the 21st century.

8. IS IT BEAUTIFUL OR ELEGANT?

No surprise here, is there? The problem is that this common desire on the part of customers aligns with the What's new? factor. People's ideas of what is beautiful or elegant keeps changing. I am not going to do much with this one, except to say that elegance is related to simplicity, which is also related to user friendliness.

9. TRUST MUST BE EARNED OVER AND OVER AGAIN

When the Atlantis of nearly every segment of society has been perceived to have been lost, trust and its companion, loyalty, become the most precious sources of success. The trust and loyalty that once seemed to be automatically accorded to the leaders of our organizations and institutions now must be earned over and over again. This is not a pleasant state of affairs. But it is a natural reaction by nearly everyone when they have seen their particular Atlantis fall from the onslaught of outside forces or due to internal decay. It is a dynamic that causes very real emotional pain for those who are consistently ethical and compassionate in dealing with others. Nevertheless, it is real and cannot be ignored. At times it seems there is zero tolerance for any error, deviation, or lapse.

A telling example, for me, of how difficult it may be for organizations to regain the trust of its employees, clients, or customers began when I received an article about "new wave QWL" (quality of worklife) from employees of a telephone company in the Midwest during the mid-1980s. I wasn't sure about accepting the article for publication because what the authors were describing as "new wave" was the starting point for most quality circles at the time. What they described as an advance didn't seem very new to me. I called one of the authors and asked as tactfully as I could, what was so new about their approach. And why, I asked, did it take them four years to start working on really significant workplace problems? (They had been working on placement of break rooms, conditions of rest rooms, and such). "First," the author said, "this represented a new step for us, we didn't mean to imply it was new for the field." Then he said that it took them four years to start working on significant work problems because, "we had seventy years of learning how to not trust management, so four years to learn that we could now trust them is not so long—is it?" I printed the article and relearned a valuable lesson. Workers are more than willing to trust that management means what is says, but they are going to test carefully whether that trust is warranted.

It goes without saying that I have relearned this lesson over and over again. I have relearned that people at every level of organizations have learned to watch the feet and not the lips of those who say, "This is not the flavor of the month, this is going to be the way we operate around here!"

What I and many others have learned is that it is much better to say, "We believe this approach will help us improve and with your help we will find out whether it does or not."

Are there concrete steps that can be taken to rebuild trust and loyalty? Sure there are, if you are able to

1. Make the assumption that the people you work with don't need to be "fixed" or educated to be trusting, and
2. You accept that those who seem to be distrustful have legitimate interests, different from yours, at stake.

Those of you who are not members of a union or who don't have a union representing your employees should not tune out the description of interest-based bargaining that follows. The process contains valuable lessons for non-union organizations because it is a vehicle to bring rational and focused discussion into arenas where there is little or no trust.

The labor relations people and many union supporters are familiar with or have at least heard about the process called *interest-based bargaining*. In my view, interest-based bargaining is not so much a trust-building process as it is a structured process within which people can openly talk about their legitimate interests and needs instead of denying the legitimacy of "opposing" sides. Trust can be and often is a by-product of the process but it is not the purpose of the process—problem solving and coming to agreement is.

Steve Barber has used this process very successfully with a large number of organizations. I highly recommend that you read his article in Chapter 9 of this book. In the last year or two, Steve found that the process or a variant of it has been quite useful in helping communities, government, and business to stop pointing fingers at each other and to work on making improvements in how communities deal with issues that range from homelessness to planning how to improve the management of watersheds.

I should also note here that several processes mentioned before, shared learning, the search conference, and participative design also deal very well with trust issues. Each process shares with the other a structured methodology which enables people to talk through issues instead of making some people wrong or right, or trying to "fix" people who are somehow "broken."

This group of methodologies and the participative frame of reference can also be used to successfully deal with trust issues between you and your

- Suppliers
- Customers
- Community
- Government (local, state, and Federal)

The main thing to act upon here is that no one is given $500 worth of trust at the start of the game anymore. You don't get any trust when you "pass go" either. Your products and services are now judged one transaction at a time. It's no different with trust.

So Where Does That Leave Us?

We have currents, rip tides, and whirlpools to overcome. These obstacles are summed up in this statement:

> I want it now, new, beautiful/elegant, high quality, low cost, earth and user friendly, and made just for me!

No problem, eh? Well, we also have managers and workers who are saying:

> "I want more input/control over my job, it should have meaning for me, I need variety/newness, I want predictability, too, I want my job to have less hassle in it/user friendliness/low cost to me, I want it to fit me, and I am going to watch your feet, not your lips!"

The traditional rock and a hard place, no?

CAN WE CREATE A BRIDGE OR FIND A PATH THROUGH THE TURBULENCE?

I said, I was going to try to create a bridge that would give us a complete management process which would help us get over the turbulence we have just spoken of. So I will. Let's begin with a picture.

Picture, if you will, that the dynamics just discussed are waves, currents, and whirlpools which are battering your organization this way and that. What you need is some type of vehicle or methodology that will take you to higher ground or at least to calmer waters. Over the past ten to fifteen years many organizations have used quality technologies and participative processes or methodologies to deal with the turbulence of their environment. The problem is this:

1. Picture quality as one foundation tower for a bridge across turbulent waters.
2. Picture participation as another such tower on the other side—solid ground.

We can (and many organizations have been been doing just this) add one piece at a time to either side and improve our position or process somewhat.

Organizations have put in statistical process control (SPC) measures, aspects of quality function deployment (QFD), and just-in-time

(JIT) concepts for dealing with suppliers. Most recently, people are adding ISO 9000 documentation and certification. Each of these additions has helped improve the organization. But in reality, each technique was still treated as if it was stand alone or an operation parallel to the "real" work of the organization.

At the same time, sometimes in the same organization, people have sought to use participative processes to improve morale, get closer to customers, improve communication, and even to problem solve. Quality control circles, self-managing teams, and task and cross-functional teams are used to enhance organizational performance in many different ways. But in reality, each technique was still treated as if they were stand alone or operations parallel to the "real" work of the organization.

In both cases, some performance is improved but overall performance still has its ups and downs. The ability of the organization to quickly and successfully adapt to its changing environment is not much affected by either approach, or even when both are going on at the same time. Some organizations have met with better success because they have made strong efforts to blend the two efforts. This is why the financial performance of organizations strongly committed to quality and participation processes is better than that of organizations which have only limited quality and limited participation processes in their organizations.

Consider what could take place if we added to these separate quality and participation processes methods and processes which would bind them all together. We'd have a bridge or process which could lead the organization through all types of rough seas or torturous terrain.

If we add to our total quality and participation processes a robust shared learning process, a strategic planning process, a participative design process, a communication planning process, and an innovation process, we have a sound group of methods which will enable us to respond rapidly and successfully to changes in our environment and we have the means to introduce environmental changes beneficial to our organization.

SO WHAT ARE THESE KEYSTONES OR CONNECTORS?

A few we have already mentioned and some will be covered at greater depth later by my co-authors. The search and participative design as developed by the Emery's and colleagues is one such key connecting methodology.

Strategic Planning and the Redesign of Work

The search conference is an excellent method to spur innovation in that it gets folks out of their old tired box via a scan of their environment that involves all those who really have knowledge of all the puzzle pieces in the organization. About 20 to 35 knowledgeable people produces a much broader perspective than that just the expert few.

The search conference is also an excellent means to develop strategies that will enable the organization to adapt in positive ways to its changing environment. It also gives the organization an experience in using a relatively fast and actively adaptive planning process that can be used over and over again—not just to adapt to the environment but to actively alter that environment as well.

Participative design takes into account the needs of both managers and workers to satisfactorily answer the question posed before: "I want more input/control over my job, it should have meaning for me, I need variety/newness, I want predictability too, I want my job to have less hassle in it/user friendliness/low cost to me, I want it to fit me as the responsible adult that I am, and I am going to watch your feet, not your lips!"

Once used, participative design can also be repeated to assist the organization to reshape itself to new needs and demands of the marketplace.

Shared Learning

Shared learning is a process similar to the search and participative design. Its strength is that it enables organizations to launch change processes simultaneously throughout the whole organization in place of the traditional "Let's try a pilot someplace and then repeat it." Shared learning gives all parts of an organization an opportunity to learn from each other as each learns or as each separately improves its processes.

Shared learning is also a process for learning within multi-site organizations and for multi-community based economic development. Tom Lyons of the Irish Productivity Centre developed this process. He has a chapter in this book and has written three articles on shared learning previously for *The Journal for Quality and Participation.*

The Innovation Cycle

I have already talked of the cycle of discontinuous, continuous, breakthrough, and again discontinuous innovation or improvement. It is enough to say here that if you don't figure out how to build such a cycle into your thinking and organizational planning cycle, you may not be in business to complete your bridge. In another sense, integration of this cycle into your culture is a way, along with the search, participative design, and shared learning, to keep rejuvenating your organization.

Communication Strategies and Planning

You and I could do everything noted above and still fail unless we have put in place communication processes and strategies which move information quickly throughout the organization. Kaat Exterbille has given this a great deal of thought and will present some guides to planning quality into your communications system.

The Participative Continuous Improvement Process

If we lived in a stable environment or even one with just two or three competitors, the participative continuous improvement (PCI) architecture outlined in Chapter 5 by Peter E. Beerten would by itself greatly enhance our ability to be the price and quality leader in our market. It stands on its own merit. But its value increases when we realize that it too is not a one-shot deal. Its value increases when we see its design and implementation as being a vital part of organizational generation, growth, and regeneration. As your product or service hits the market and causes it to shift in a discontinuous manner, you must realize that in short order, your customers will want to see improvements. Therefore, you apply the PCI process to that product. And so it goes through each step of the innovation cycle.

An Example of Applying All of These Methodologies

Let's ask this question: If an organization launched a new product two years ago, how might they now use these methodologies to enhance overall organizational performance, improve the bottom line, and enhance their ability to create a successful future for themselves?

1. The innovation cycle concept is shared and disseminated throughout the whole organization—long-term success for every employee and the organization as a whole depends on their innovation ability.

Since they have launched the new product two years ago, they have made some modifications and improvements, but they now have three competitors who have entered their market with similar products.

2. They decide to use the breakthrough quality methodology contained within a shared learning process to create large service and product improvements within six months. Before implementation they will use both the search conference and participative design processes to redesign work processes and flows where appropriate.
3. Pre-planning begins with a search conference that will focus on creating a discontinuous improvement that will reshape their market within 16 to 24 months.

4. Communications planning and design is applied to both the break-through and discontinuous improvement processes.
5. Participative continuous improvement processes are introduced via a shared learning process to all support operations. Their collective goal is to substantially improve their support of employees in direct contact with customers so that front-line employees can focus more time and attention on those customers and less energy and time on negotiating for resources and support from their organization.

This is only one example, but I think it demonstrates how all of these methodologies can support each other and the organization's ability to become more adaptable as well as more proactive in their environment. Another advantage of being able to call upon all of these processes and having them embedded into your work, leadership, and management systems is that they can also be used to improve each other and thus improve again your ability to improve and adapt.

THE FLEXIBLE AND SELF-AWARE ORGANIZATION

Now that you have the idea of building bridges firmly in mind, I invite you to drop the analogy for a bit. Taken too far, the notion of a bridge can lead us to think that our human systems can be engineered in the same manner as machines. To survive in turbulent times organizations must

- Be open enough to take in information from as many sources as possible.
- Have an ability to quickly process new information and to disseminate subsequent learning quickly to all of its subsystems.
- Be solid and disciplined enough to transform that learning into high-quality products, services, and processes.

In short, they have to be able to flow like a raging river, float like a leaf, and steer a course like a world-class windsurfer. (Leaping tall buildings we will leave to Superman and Superwoman.) There are three key characteristics enhancing these organizational abilities:

1. The participation of everyone in the success of the organization.
2. The free flow of information and communication throughout the organization.
3. Creating an environment in which everyone in the organization is encouraged and enabled to push themselves to higher levels of performance. (This third key will be examined in greater depth in Chapter 2.)

The focus necessary to activate these keys is quality. Increasing or enhancing communication, participation, and challenge each for their own sake will, in the long run, have no more effect than a well-planned pep rally. When the cheering is all over, you must successfully complete your tasks on your own. A focus on improving the quality of your processes, products, and services creates a synergy that is explosive in its power.

Why Focus on Quality?

The elusiveness of a once and for all definition for quality is its strength. It has a pulling and pushing effect of all those who seek to improve it. Quality serves the same function to an organization that the concept of freedom or democracy does to society at large. The search for operational definitions and applications of freedom, democracy, or quality change and grow as society changes or as new generations look about themselves and their environment and decide that it could be better. If there were hard and fast definitions for any of these concepts, the danger would be that entropy would then set in and we would decline and fall as did the Atlantis of legend.

The Breadth and Depth of Quality

The breadth or scope of quality describes who is involved, what functions are involved, and what tools are used in the quality process. The depth of quality describes how much discretion and authority people have to improve quality, how much information and training they have, and how the customer defines quality over time.

This search for the meaning and application of the breadth and depth of quality in your organization, more than what new team or quality process is in vogue today, will shape the future of how you deal with turbulence. Does marketing have a role in quality improvement? Yes. Does employee involvement and quality have a role in safety? Yes. In pollution prevention? Yes.

When people begin to understand that the pursuit of the breadth and depth of quality will lead to understanding that the possible extinction of a plant or animal may be presenting us with a symptom that something is amiss in our mutual survival system, they will be ready to tap into the most amazing source of innovation and satisfaction we could imagine.

Some Closing Thoughts

To take us from the 30,000 foot view to the 5′ 8″ view, let's look again at the expectations of the typical customer and employee. She or he has

- An expectation of low price, high quality
- A desire for more control of processes

- The desire for something new
- The desire for something which not only works but expresses his or her individuality

Whether you are producing cars, computers, or delivering business services or meals, this combination of expectations and desires is both your blessing and fate.

> Thrive on it and you will succeed. Ignore it and risk grieving over the passing of your organization and job.

The nine dynamics described in this chapter constantly drive change and turbulence. There are other drivers of change, to be sure but these have the most immediate impact on your organization and they appear to be the ones over which you have the greatest potential to influence to your benefit.

Two things we can be sure of are that none of these dynamics will go away and they will all keep moving. If the targets keep moving, we'd better figure out how to either keep up or make new targets.

I invite you now, to read on in this book and consider how the methodologies and approaches of my colleagues will help you work, manage, and lead successfully in our turbulent times.

Ned Hamson is currently the senior editor of *The Journal for Quality and Participation.* The journal is published by the Association for Quality and Participation (headquarters in Cincinnati, Ohio). Mr. Hamson has been the editor of the association's journal and its newsletter since December 1985.

The Journal for Quality and Participation features articles by organizations which are using total quality and participation processes to improve quality, customer satisfaction, labor-management relations, and productivity. His duties as editor have brought him into close contact with leading organizations, consultants, and practitioners in the quality and participation field. Fred and Merrelyn Emery, Armand V. Feigenbaum, Phil Crosby, Tom Peters, Dr. Deming, Dr. Juran, Dr, Ishikawa, Jim Harrington, Jean Houston, Margaret Wheatley, Pat Townsend, Peter Senge, Dr. Chris Argyris, Russ Ackoff, Paul Allaire, Roger Smith, Fred Smith, and Presidents Bush and Clinton are just a few of those who have written for *The Journal for Quality and Participation* while Mr. Hamson has been its editor.

Prior to joining the AQP, Mr. Hamson was the administrative assistant and legislative assistant to two different City of Cincinnati council members from 1974 to 1985. Prior to those positions, he held a variety of positions in both the public and private sector.

Mr. Hamson holds a B.A. from the School of International Service at American University in Washington, DC and a M.A. from the University of Cincinnati. Both degrees were in political economy with special emphasis in international affairs, economics, and public administration.

Mr. Hamson also conducted extensive research on political economy during his attendance at the University of the Seven Seas (now World Campus Afloat) in 1966. His research (supported by a scholarship) at this university was conducted in: Tahiti, New Zealand, Australia, Singapore, India, Sri Lanka, Kenya, Lebanon, Somalia, Egypt, Israel, Greece, Italy, Algiers, Morocco, and Madeira.

To learn more about the Association for Quality and Participation call: 800-733-3310, 513-381-1959, or E-mail aqp@aqp2.org

EDITOR'S NOTE:

Have you ever been a part of one of the following experiences or one like it? Or have you seen one of these in a television report?

- A group of strangers suddenly becomes a high-performing team as they attempt to pull a young couple out of an overturned car on the side of the highway.
- Habitat for Humanity workers who have never lifted a hammer seem to know just where to be and what to do as they work together to build homes in rural and urban areas. The look in their eyes and the sounds of their voices make you think of a party rather than hard work.
- The crew of people serving meals to the homeless and cleaning up afterward look as though they are flowing in their work and enjoying it, apart from being satisfied they are helping others.
- The people who struggle to create a new sandbag levee just in time to save several homes from a rising river look as though they are the hands and feet of one person, one mind. Apart from the satisfaction of saving the homes, some seem almost embarrassed to acknowledge that the experience was very enjoyable.

Did you say or did someone else say: "I wish I could always work this way," or "Why can't people work and care like this all of the time?"

Frank Heckman says, "We can work this way." We can work this way, Heckman says because we can now combine what have been separate areas of research on optimal performance/experience (flow) and practical applications of open systems theory (the search conference and participative design). The added bonus, Heckman says, is that by combining these concepts and methods, we produce organizations which are better able to adapt themselves successfully to the ever-changing requirements of our turbulent environment.

Chapter 2

Designing Organizations for Flow and Adaptability

Frank Heckman, Frank Heckman Consulting

T here is a name for the experience when people are so focused that it amounts to absolute absorption in an activity, providing a sense of discovery, a creative feeling of pushing to higher levels of performance—into a new reality. The experience is called . . . FLOW!

> "It usually began when three or four of the guys on the floor would heat up . . . The feeling would spread to other guys, and we'd all levitate . . . The game would be in the white heat of competition, and yet I never felt the pain.
>
> My premonitions would be consistently correct . . . There have been many times in my career that I felt moved or happy, but these were moments when I had chills pulsing up and down my spine."
>
> —BILL RUSSELL

Few of us can share the pro basketball experience of Michael Jordan, or the way Bill Russell describes the pressures of the game. Yet many work situations can, under the right circumstances, provide both great challenge and intense satisfaction, with the same sense of cohesion, accomplishment, and control which can occur during a pro basketball game. Listen, for example, to what this technical support group from a large consulting firm has to say:

> "We had ten weeks to complete the project, and started two weeks late. Our objectives were quite clear and through the high-level complexity

27

of the project, our group was forced into a continuous learning and solution seeking mode. Despite the tremendous pressures, we were pretty soon in the groove of collaboratively and effectively deciding on all sorts of issues all the time, moving through and around the obstacles with great conviction and a sense that nothing could stop us. We came to call our project 'mission impossible,' and upon completion, many of us confessed that this had been one of the most exciting and best experiences in our professional life."

BETWEEN BOREDOM AND ANXIETY THERE EXISTS A ZONE WHERE CREATIVE POTENTIAL MAY BE REALIZED

Flow is the result of a ground breaking study conducted by Mihalyi Csikszentmihalyi[1] (University of Chicago). Csikszentmihalyi conducted extensive research, interviewing more than 8,000 people all over the world to distinguish what makes for an enjoyable *flow experience.*

He found that, whether it concerned teenagers in Tokyo, steelworkers in Gary, Indiana, farmers in Northern Italy, or fishermen in Korea, people achieve a form of happiness *(a state of flow),* when they pursue attainable but challenging goals.

When people approach challenging physical and/or mental tasks matched with high personal skill, they not only enjoy the experience,

Flow . . . A state of consciousness so focused that it amounts to absolute absorption in an activity. It provides a sense of discovery, a creative feeling of pushing to higher levels of performance— into a new reality.

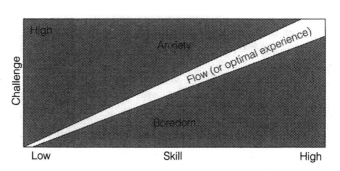

Figure 2.1 Flow: Between boredom and anxiety

---

[1] Csikszentmihalyi is a professor and former chairman of the department of psychology at the University of Chicago.

they stretch their capabilities and increase the likelihood that they will learn or achieve new and higher skill levels and increase their self esteem.

Flow Isn't Just an Enjoyable Experience

Through focusing attention and overcoming a challenge, we are changed—we end up feeling more capable and looking forward to overcoming new challenges. As Csikszentmihalyi quotes a rock climber as saying, "You look back at yourself, at what you've done, it just blows your mind."

Too Great a Challenge Can Produce Anxiety, Too Little, Boredom

If, despite the tension and challenge, a person believes she or he can succeed, the act of struggling in single-minded fashion to overcome the challenge elicits strong feelings of satisfaction, creativity, clear-mindedness, power, control, concentration, and enjoyment.

Flow Is Intrinsically Rewarding

The key element of a flow experience is that even if initially undertaken for other reasons, the activity becomes intrinsically rewarding. Csikszentmihalyi calls this an autotelic experience (*auto* meaning self and *telos* meaning goal). For example, teaching children math is not in and of itself an autotelic experience. The feeling you have (due to your ongoing efforts) when they are all busily engaged in learning new skills and not running amok can definitely be an autotelic experience.

While we might expect that such experiences happen most often during play, romantic, or creative experiences, Csikszentmihalyi found that the place where this flow state occurred most frequently was at work!! The most relevant point here is this:

> When the match between perceived challenge and personal skill is intrinsically gratifying, employees are naturally motivated to seek out such opportunities and continue to learn.

How does all this match up with the dark side of the story about work which says: "in our fast-paced society more and more people are falling victim to being tense or worried during their work, showing a dramatic increase in physical illnesses and psychiatric symptoms of distress?" Is there reason to remain optimistic?

Flow Occurs with Surprising Consistency

Remarkably, the research on flow shows with surprising consistency that people have not lost their ability to find happiness and meaning in the challenges that face them in the workplace! There are quite a few people who seem to have a canny ability to seek out possibilities for autotelic action, even in the least favorable circumstances.

Is Flow More Than a Bonus, Does It Serve a Purpose?

It now seems likely that flow has something to do with how we humans have evolved. Stuart Kauffman, a pioneer in the science of complexity, indicates that Darwin's view of the survival of the fittest (humans had larger brains, thus they were fitter than other species) is too easy an explanation. Kauffman suggests a broader evolutionary path:

> "Complex systems that exist on the boundary between order and chaos are the most likely to evolve. They have somehow acquired the ability to bring order and chaos into a special kind of balance. On this edge of chaos is where life has enough stability to sustain itself and enough creativity to deserve the name of life. The edge of chaos is where new ideas and innovative genotypes are forever nibbling away at the edges of the status quo, and where the most entrenched old guard will eventually be overthrown."

Following this line of thought, it is probably more than a coincidence that the potential for quantum change in physical systems, described by chemists and biologists as existing on the boundary between chaos and order, bears a strong resemblance to the complex psychic state of flow that exists on the boundary between boredom and anxiety. In both cases the evolution of new properties or traits and skills proceeds more rapidly at the edge of order and chaos.

Csikszentmihalyi talks about the boundary condition as not only essential but as a preferred condition:

> "That we enjoy being on the boundary seems a gift from providence; it could almost be interpreted that humans have a vocation for evolution. But it is more likely that all living things—or at least those that will evolve—prefer to dwell on that precarious boundary."

Are We Wired for Flow and Adaptation?

As humans, we have a need to set ourselves apart, to be appreciated for who we are as individuals, but we also have a deep need to affiliate, to belong to, to be part of the group. Living in a society that places strong emphasis on the individual contribution, we tend to forget that the greatest development of the human race has come from how we evolved—together!

The view of Darwinists and neo-Darwinists is that our ancestors were at a great disadvantage living in a wilderness under continuous threat of death from stronger, faster, and bigger predators. Supposedly, the only reason our ancestors survived (as the fittest) was because of their large brains and their ability to use tools. Today we are coming to the understanding that our foraging ancestors had an innate ability to create complex, close-knit social groupings and that this ability, much more than the making of tools, accounts for the development of the large brain.

Most of our historical experience has been structured around flow, learning and adapting together. Before the advent of agriculture and later urbanized living, for 98% of our existence on the planet, we worked together as groups of hunter-gatherer bands. Our ancestors had a rich emotional and sophisticated social life, surviving and thriving in circumstances and environments in which modern man wouldn't last very long.

Charles Ehin, professor at the Gore Business School, Westminster College in Salt Lake City notes:

> "The social organization of our ancestors in small nomadic bands, clustered around tribal communities, could provide some of the desperately needed knowledge to reshape ourselves, our work, organizations, and institutions today."

According to Canadian anthropologist Richard Lee, who has studied the !Kung Bushman:[2]

> "The ancient, time-tested strategies for the exploitation of a broad spectrum of local food resources effectively shatters the long-standing anthropological myth that the so-called 'hunting and gathering' way of life—to date as the most successful, persistent adaptation man has ever achieved and a way of life that was, until the dawn of agriculture some 10,000 years ago, the universal mode of human existence—was exceedingly grim and precarious, accompanied by chronic hunger and misery."

> "Despite the austerity of their landscapes, the adults in the community can reliably meet the basic subsistence needs of their nomad population, which includes a high proportion of dependent young and elderly members, by each devoting an estimated twelve to nineteen hours per week—about six hundred to a thousand hours per year—to the quest for food."

Not a bad balance when compared to the quality of work life and home life of modern urbanites.

---

[2] The !Kung Bushman in Northeastern Botswana are one of the last indigenous tribes on the planet living as hunters and gathers, although fewer of them still solely rely on it.

Hunter-gatherer communities were highly adaptive. The social fabric of our minds has evolved for a great part of our existence in a society roaming about in small bands. The notion of responsible group self-direction in our past puts the autotelic experience of flow in a social context. The continuing dynamic situation in which the tribe has to pull all possible resources together to respond and adapt adequately to drought, hostilities from other tribes, seasons, threats of predators, and dangers of the hunt, as well as opportunities for culture, health, and overall well-being is the ideal context to break through outlived patterns by producing and re-experiencing flow.

Flow at Work?

It still seems surprising to find that people experience flow much more at work than anywhere else. Csikszentmihalyi explains that the part of our life that we call work lends itself better to flow. The essential components, or conditions to flow, despite the drawbacks we commonly experience, occur more often in the structured, task-oriented world of work:

- Clear goals
- Immediate feedback
- Challenges which match skills
- Areas where action and awareness merge

Without question, flow as the preferred state of mind has a greater likelihood to emerge in an environment in which people have more freedom of choice into how to apply themselves. When a structure of enforced demands and enforced isolation gives way to an environment where expression and function are more balanced, flow becomes part of the natural order of things, a predisposition waiting to be triggered.

SO WHY DOESN'T MY WORK FLOW—FOR ME, OR FOR MY WORK GROUP?

A short review of how the dominant organizational forms of the last 200 years will give us an answer and also explain today's gap between how we are structured for work and the reality of the vastly changing environments in which we exist.

Newton and Taylor Were Fine In 1900 but Fail To Pass the Test for the Year 2000

The dawning of the steam-driven Machine Age was driven in large part by a science drawn from Newton's clockwork view of the universe. It was based on breaking things down into their smallest components and understanding movement or power as controlled action and reaction. Fritzjof Capra, author of *The Turning Point* writes:

> "Without question Newton has made a giant contribution to physics, taught us all about building machines . . . but very little about life."

While such analysis enabled people to create machines which could reliably stamp out thousands of the same product, when this analysis was applied to organizing people to build and operate those machines, a critical error was made. The error was this: Unlike machines, people learn and learn even better together.

Following the *break-things-down-to-their-smallest-part* paradigm, Frederick Taylor, the father of *Scientific Management,* insisted that increasing work productivity by demanding that more and faster work could only be done by isolating workers, or they would either revolt against the process or return to time-wasting socializing. The situation of enforced demands combined with enforced isolation is in itself a unique and rare approach to work, contrary to the psychological needs of people, risking their esteem and sense of self-worth.

The breakdown of work into its smallest component established a work environment in which one didn't have to rely on people. Tightly defined and controlled jobs made it easy to replace people at any given moment—people were expendable. Needless to say, this kind of workplace wasn't (and isn't) helping people much to experience flow at work. Nevertheless, when the main focus was on growing production for relatively stable markets and moving large numbers of people with little education or low technical skills into the workplace, the machine model of a people organization generated tremendous wealth. Indeed, it seemed to work well for a long time during the Industrial Era.

Since the mid-1950s, however, the world has shifted from one that could be characterized as a segmented pie of stable markets to one that today resembles a roiling, boiling cauldron of hyperkinetic forces, events, and uncertain relations.

As we face a world of permanent turbulent reality at the door to the next century, it's clear that the lifeless, clockwork machine model no longer delivers the goods or lifestyle we desire. On this threshold, the 200 years of Newtonian vision and nearly 100 years of being organized by Taylor's isolated human machine doesn't die easy and seems, at times, to offer a false stability, perhaps a golden age that could be regained and preserved.

Two Evolutionary Choices for Organizing Ourselves

The perspective of Michael Chance from the Social Systems Institute in Birmingham, England should help us see our way back to flow as worth the risk of transforming our work systems and our system of organizing work. He says that our social life and corresponding mentality are constructed on relatively simple underlying frameworks upon which we weave our affairs. Chance says we have evolved in response to the demands of our social existence. This evolution, he notes, consists of the interplay or tension between "two antithetical types of social system with markedly different thrusts." "In our evolutionary history," he says, "we tend to function in one of the two mental modes:"

- In the *agonic mode,* people are concerned most with self-security. Attention is taken up with being part of a group and with what others think of us so as to assure acceptance by the group. People are concerned with rank hierarchy, convention, and maintaining good order, as an expression of this inbred security mechanism. In the agonic mode, people's concerns are predominantly self-protective

---

Examples of the agonic and hedonic modes of organizing and experiencing work

Chance says we have evolved in response to the demands of our social existence. This evolution, he notes, consists of the interplay or tension between "two antithetical types of social system with markedly different thrusts." "In our evolutionary history," he says, "we tend to function in one of the two mental modes."

One firm: two modes of work:

The hunter–gatherer hedonic mode: The purchasing division of one of the larger insurance firms in the U.S. had just undergone a facelift to become more autonomous. It operates as its own profit–and–loss center, has few levels of decision making, information is open and accessible, groups have been formed around work processes, and people have the skills and tools to analyze and make decisions about their own work. The environment in which these people worked had an openness that was charged with intentions and enthusiasm as a result of all the recent changes. In this socially supportive work environment people had enough elbow room to make decisions about their own work and a high frequency of work related flow was noted. People reported: "I clearly know what I'm supposed to do. I feel can handle the demands of the situation. My work is important to me and I would do it even if I didn't have to. I don't get distracted too much. I feel good about myself."

The clockwork agonic mode: In a traditional print shop in the same company, with a one man–one job fragmentation of labor and many layers of decision making, hardly any flow was found related to work. People in the print shop did indeed have flow experiences but mostly outside their work in hobbies, with family, or even driving their car.

and we engage information processing systems that are specifically designed to attend, recognize, and respond to potential threats to our physical self, status, and social presentation."

- "In the *hedonic mode* (typical of nomadic cultures)," Chance says, "we are more free to form a network of personal relationships that typically offer mutual support . . . we . . . give free rein to our intelligence, our creativity, and the creation of systems of order in our thought and social relations." This, Chance says, is "because attention when released from self-protective needs, can be used to explore and integrate many new domains."

ISN'T THERE A CONFLICT BETWEEN INDIVIDUAL AUTONOMY AND GROUP DECISION MAKING OVER FLOW?

Anthropologist Margaret Power explains the difference between our notion of autonomy and that of the hunter-gatherer:

> "Our idea of autonomy is to withstand the social pressures for conformity and act independently, in contrast, for our foraging ancestors autonomy is experienced as a state in which responsible self-direction is expected as a structural property of the group. It does not imply the rejection of group norms, but rather, within the necessary roles individuals are free to make their own choices, to take part or not take part in any activity, to choose whether or not be organized by others and by which others, to join or not to join. These choices lead to a high level of 'independent conformity'—not to be confused by obedience (behavior regulated by a higher authority)."

Looking for Ways To Organize Work for Flow and Adaptability

The snapshot from the insurance firm's purchasing department reveals that certain conditions, policies, and structures are conducive to flow. This is encouraging, but insufficient to fulfill the quest for a workplace or work group that not only makes the flow experience possible but shows us that the flow experience will occur again and again. In other words, a workplace or work group that has the capacity to evolve and develop its human potential over the course of time will succeed.

These are the same questions that the Tavistock Institute for Industrial Relations in England was grappling with 50 years ago. Observing how the coal industry in Yorkshire was struggling with the problem of incorporating new digging technology helped Tavistock researchers Bamforth, Trist, and Emery understand that individual work groups are perfectly capable of dealing with significant changes in their work environment.

Active Adaptation and Open Systems Theory

In 1951, at the Haigmoor, a British coal mine, a group of miners are observed discussing the next job. By taking stock of and pooling their physical abilities, skills, and resources, they prepare themselves for yet another day in their risky world of mining coal deep under the South Yorkshire landscape:

- They prepare for the day's work not by focusing on single tasks, but on getting the whole job done.
- They talk about using the full repertoire of skills that each has and how they will interchangeably do all that needs to be done that day—from shoring up walls to extracting and moving coal and all the planning that comes with it.
- At the end of the week, after each worker receives their week's pay packet, they put their money on the table and redistribute the pay according to their own work design and schedules.

Their production and cost management is impressive and dramatically better than similar mining operations elsewhere. Cooperation was the preferred way of working, absenteeism was low, morale and commitment were high, and accidents were infrequent. Australian social scientist Fred Emery who later joined K.W. Bamforth and Eric Trist on the Haigmoor project, says of what he witnessed: "We knew that the small, self-managing work group held the key to a very great deal that might be improved in work organizations."

Open Systems Theory and Active Adaptive Human Organizations

At the Haigmoor Mine, Trist and Emery saw groups of people dealing quite effectively with a rapidly changing environment and groups that were unable to deal well with such change. The difference was how the group managed itself and adapted to the needs of each day.

By 1965, their continued research enabled them to publish a ground-breaking article that laid out a spectrum of environments from random to stable to turbulent. They found that as the environment became more and more turbulent (increases in uncertainty and complexity of the world), it made sense for organizations to act as what was known in biology as an *open system*.

Emery notes that by relocating responsibility for control and coordination to the actual level of work, organizations can begin to operate as an open system, which maximizes the flexibility and adaptive potential of all its members.

In 1965, Emery and Trist rang the bell for the last round of the bureaucratic organization—its closed, introverted, top down perspective would no longer be able to sustain itself in a vastly changing and highly demanding world.

Their open systems perspective of human organizations went beyond biologist Von Bertalanffy's general systems theory which stated that systems simply exchange energy and matter to survive. People, Trist and Emery said, don't just passively adapt to the changes in the environment; they are systems with their own purposes, and they constantly learn from and act upon their environments.

People, they said, live within a set of relationships determined by:

- The individual
- The work group
- The system or organization
- The environment, including society at large

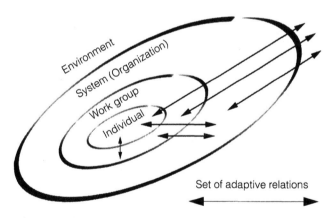

The world in which we live today has dynamics that are much more powerful than the particular needs and desires of any one organization, regardless of its size or present market-share. Microsoft is, in a sense, king of the hill in the world of computer software but in nearly every interview, CEO Bill Gates says his firm must continue to adapt to or anticipate the needs of its customers because in six months they could be out of date and headed downhill.

The key is to look at the dynamics and events in the environment and find out how they relate to each other and how they can help the business. Open systems thinking urges each of us to puzzle through the different sets of relationships, leading to a radically different way of learning, planning, and organizing.

Figure 2.2   Open systems thinking is key to organizational adaptability

Emery and Trist's open systems approach is the opposite of reductionist problem solving or linear extension of past and present thinking into the future. The world in which we live today has dynamics that are much more powerful than the particular needs and desires of any one organization, regardless of its size or present marketshare. Microsoft is, in a sense, king of the hill in the world of computer software but in nearly every interview, CEO Bill Gates says his firm must continue to adapt to or anticipate the needs of its customers because in six months they could be out of date and headed downhill.

The key is to look at the dynamics and events in the environment and find out how they relate to each other and how they can help the business. Open systems thinking urges each of us to puzzle through the different sets of relationships, leading to a radically different way of learning, planning, and organizing.

Organizing Human Systems for Adaptability

Emery's involvement in the Industrial Democracy Project in Norway during the mid-1960s proved to him that democracy was a viable alternative to autocracy and especially suited to work in turbulent environments. Shortly after returning home, Emery was confronted with a great need and demand in Australia for renewing organizations—he and Merrelyn Emery went to work.

Applications of Open Systems Theory to the Workplace

Fred Emery formulated a new method, based on open systems theory, for creating actively adaptive, democratic workplaces which he called the *participative design workshop*. Emery explains his approach in this manner:

> "The expert driven change methodologies (such as re-engineering) continue the tired old concept of designing the technical system first and force-fitting the social system into it. Once the responsibility is put back where the work is done, people themselves will take responsibility for making the technical system work. That means you change the social structure of work first and as a result everything else changes."

In the participative design workshop, the people who do the work design the work. When the workshop is preceded by a search conference[3] (a participative strategic planning process) people are able to achieve full,

---

[3] Begun by Fred Emery and Eric Trist and fully developed by Merrelyn Emery

Design Principle One

Design principle one produces a bureaucratic organization where responsibility for coordination and control are located one level above where the work is being done.

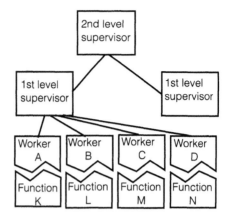

Design Principle Two

Design principle two produces a democratic organization in which people are skilled in a wide variety of social and technical tasks and functions. The structure will take the form of a self–managing team that is responsible for the control and coordination of its own work.

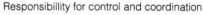

Responsibillity for control and coordination

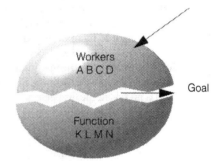

Figure 2.3 Design Principle

active adaptation between themselves, their work, organization and the environment. Emery's two design principles portray two forms of work organization:

1. The conventional, self-enveloped, spare parts type of structure
2. The self-managing, adaptive group structure

Shifting responsibility for coordination and control to where the work is actually done marks a radical difference in attitude and mentality about how people approach their work.

Emery's great contribution is his insight that the perceived threats to the individual at work actually reside in the organizational structure! The perceived threats he identified are:

- No elbow room
- Lack of challenge to learn

The six human requirements for productive activity:

1. *Adequate elbow room for decision making.* The sense that people can influence their own work and that, with the exception of specific circumstances, they don't have to ask permission for everything. Enough elbow room to feel empowered but not so much that they do not know what to do. (Notice the similarity here to the requirements for flow in work.)
2. *Opportunity to learn continually on the job.* Such learning is possible when people can set goals that are reasonable challenges for them and get timely feedback on results.
3. *An optimum level of variety.* Through the avoidance of boredom and fatigue, people can gain the best advantages from settling into a satisfying and effective rhythm of work.
4. *Mutual support and respect.* Conditions where people can and do get help and respect from their co–workers.
5. *Meaningfulness.* A sense of one's own work meaningfully contributing to society. Also, to have knowledge of the whole product or service. Many jobs lack meaningfulness, because workers see only such a small part of the final product that meaning is denied to them.
6. *A desirable future.* Put simply, not a dead end job, but one with a career path which will allow personal growth and increase in skills.

- Repetitive work without variety
- The absence of mutual support and respect
- The denial of meaning in work
- A lack of perspective or future

The *design principle one* structure has an inverse relationship with what Emery calls the six human requirements for productive activity.

Identifying these very human requirements as critical to productive work is the result of cumulative worldwide research on what motivates people to put their best foot forward at work. Once these requirements are met by applying the second design principle, the creative intelligence and cooperative potential in people surfaces and comes alive. At the same time, through optimizing the organizational structure for these human requirements, the potential for flow experiences rises exponentially.

The outcome of the participative search and (re)design is a flexible, actively adaptive organization, structured around multi-skilled, self-managing groups. The work group becomes the primary building block on all organizational dimensions, from finance to research, marketing to the sales room or shop floor.

Art Kleiner, author of *The Age of Heretics,* tells the story of how this way of organizing work is so powerful that in one case, four sets of management couldn't kill it:

> "An idea rooted in a dog food factory that four different companies have owned, enjoyed great results from, and then try to shut it down—only to have the idea bite management back. The experiment with Emery and Trist's workplace democracy ideas housed in a gleaming white silo-shaped plant on the Kansas prairie in Topeka. Sections of the plant painted in bright colors became natural centers where teams gravitated to compare notes—or to thrash out differences.
>
> There were no supervisors, only teams and team members who controlled plant operations. They hired new members, assigned shifts, set hours, and redesigned the placement of machinery. Everyone rotated through a wide variety of jobs. Significantly, they freely shared information about the plant's finances and cash flow. Without the overhead of a supervisory level, with an astonishing low 2% absentee rate, and with a level of involvement bordering on ownership, the Topeka plant set records at General Foods. Then corporate managers withdrew their support and declared the experiment 'out of control' and put a new manager in place to 'cut out the missionary crap.'
>
> Too late. The system had already taken on a life of its own. Three owners down the line, Heinz acquired the plant in 1995 and it looked as if the new owners, after all the other previous attempts, might finally put the experiment to sleep. But the team-based structure refused to roll over and play dead. Today Heinz says: 'The system in Topeka has evolved to a much higher level than any of our other plants. We look at it as a model of where we'd like to go."

SOME CLOSING THOUGHTS ON FLOW, ADAPTATION, AND DEMOCRACY

If we assume that all living things, including humans, have a vocation for evolution, then being poised on the edge of the 21st century just might be the challenge we need. The increasing turmoil of this decade and the dynamics of our shrinking world have stirred up a broad conversation about how we work together, expand individual freedom, create opportunities for strengthening our families and communities, and increase our knowledge about our world and our ability to positively influence our future in it.

Perhaps the yearning many of us have for a better experience at work is really our collective conscience whispering to each of us:

"When the new millennium arrives, how will we measure up? What have we become? Will we build a positive future with our creativity and resources, or will we be the first of the last generation?"

These pressures and questions should help us to remember our genetic, evolutionary disposition and realize that it is quite natural for us to work together effectively. The history of our world teaches us that when individuals and groups of people come together, they are capable of pushing the boundaries and overcoming unbelievable challenges. We have only to think of the people who accepted the challenge of putting the first man on the moon, or those with the vision of providing every household with a personal computer.

On an individual level we each have our own flow experiences from the time we first ride our bicycle to solving a complex math problem. There are countless examples of athletes, inventors, entrepreneurs, and personal heroes or mentors who model flow experiences. On the small group level, we know about the technical support group or the British miners that can be found working together with the same kind of flow, learning, and excitement.

Since the 1950s, when Bamforth and Trist stumbled upon this group of coal miners at the Haigmoor, the methods for creating productive democratic organizations have been well developed by Fred and Merrelyn Emery and their colleagues around the world. What is really encouraging and exciting is that more and more people today, including complexity theorists, are beginning to discover that democracy is not a political agenda but an integral part of the natural order of things and is perhaps the most sensible way to achieve the best attainable solutions among conflicting practical, political, and moral interests!

As hundreds of organizations worldwide apply this open systems approach to planning and designing work, it is apparent that this is not only a human and pragmatic way for the individual and their organizations to get organized, it also allows for fulfillment of the creative potential of people by setting the stage for flow experiences.

In the two sections that follow, I will demonstrate in greater depth, through a community search conference, how people in all types of organizations can participatively and innovatively plan their future and how they can organize themselves to achieve that future.

THE SEARCH CONFERENCE DELIVERS ON ITS PROMISE TO HELP PEOPLE PLAN CHALLENGING AND EXCITING FUTURES

The results from using the search conference as a regional planning process by the Macatawa area (the cities of Holland, Zeeland, and five adjoining Michigan townships) prove that democratic planning is alive, effective, and working well in the U.S.

On a sunny May morning in 1995, 110 people are gathering in Christ Memorial church in Holland, Michigan to attend the First Annual participative follow-up to the Macatawa Search Conference.[4] The agenda for the day is to review the last year's achievements, reassess the long range desired future for Macatawa, and to establish priorities for the coming year.

The stage was set for this day a year earlier when 63 citizens of the 7 municipalities that make up the Macatawa area gathered for a three-day search conference in Big Rapids. This initial search conference established a jointly determined vision for a desired future for the area and a plan to implement it.

During the search, priority groups planned, involved other initiatives and people, and began the journey to reach their objectives. The 1994 plan was adopted as both the regional strategic plan and led to the creation of a new organizational form for the Macatawa regional council. By the end of that search conference, participants agreed to work together to improve the quality of life in the Greater Macatawa Area through creative, cooperative, and comprehensive work in the following areas:

- Economic development
- Lifelong learning
- Environment
- Personal safety
- Health care
- Residential life
- Land use and transportation
- Social services

Today (May 1995) people are gathering together to celebrate the accomplishments of a year's commitment. The large meeting space is transformed into a science-fair-like exhibition complete with visual displays, videos, and an array of other artifacts. Eight priority action groups are presenting the year's accomplishments along with stories of how they

---

[4] Rather than being a new search, this was a follow-up search to the first search.

overcame obstacles. At the same time, the action groups are, in turn, getting plenty of feedback on their work through small group discussions.

Macatawa's Environmental Action Team Report

Greg Holcombe from the Environmental Action Team explains: "We defined our purpose on the environment to initiate actions to identify and preserve sensitive and unique natural features and properties within the Greater Lake Macatawa watershed for public enjoyment, use, and accessibility. The overall goal of this effort is to create and protect a Greenway Network in the Macatawa region. This network will be an interconnected system of public and private parks, forests, streams, and other open, undeveloped lands. These areas will be connected along Lake Macatawa tributaries by greenways which will provide corridors for use by citizens and wildlife."

Holcombe continues: "Inspired by the great parks and open spaces in this country such as Grant Park, Lincoln Park, the Forest Preserve in Chicago, Fairmont Park in Philadelphia, and the Boston Public Garden, our first goal was to map all the property that would compose the aspired Greenway Network." Holcombe then pointed to the large Macatawa Greenway Network map they constructed during the year. "Our next challenge," Holcombe said, "was to determine how these core properties would be formed into the Network by interconnecting them with Macatawa river tributaries. Fortunately, many of these mapped properties are already afforded long-term protection through their present use—such as parklands, school uses, and to a degree, most of the Macatawa River streambanks. The group's current goal is to continue identifying property owners and discussing possible agreements, land sales, etc. This summer we will set some model agreements. Simultaneously, city councils and other policy boards have been made aware and are asked for input."

You may be saying to yourself now, "This sounds like any planners report; what's the big deal?" The essential difference is that Mr. Holcombe is not a professional planner—he is a volunteer. To help you understand how this action planning group was able to make such progress, some background and understanding of the search conference process is in order.

WHAT IS A COMMUNITY SEARCH CONFERENCE?

The search conference is a participative planning method in which people create a plan for the most desirable future of their community. During a search conference, some 20-50 citizens (community leaders, businessmen and women, parents, and workers) become a learning/planning community. Together they create a vision, develop action plans and strategies, and agree to stick with it all the way through implementation.

How Is this Approach Different from Other Planning Approaches?

The search conference method is based on the clear understanding that our social environment has made a radical shift from being relatively stable to being highly dynamic and unpredictable. Strategic planning, tactical and operational sessions which assume that the future can be created by extrapolating the past into the future are obsolete. Plans based upon linear projections from historical data are bound to falter, as they meet with the unpredictable and fast-changing present. The search conference has been researched, tested, and designed to help organizations quickly adapt to changing environments.

Search conference underpinnings: its theory, values, and philosophy assume people have the ability to plan their future.

- Participation is equal and open (leave your hat at the door). All ideas are valid.
- It is democratic by design, people are responsible for the control and coordination of their own work.
- Explores how the surrounding world, with all its changes, forces, and uncertainties, affects the community or region (reality checkpoint for future planning). Remembers the past, evaluates the present, and creates a preferred future to end with a plan that is:
- Realistically balanced between the assets of the community and its (ever) changing environment
- Focuses on future possibilities
- Has no presenters, lectures, keynote addresses, games, or training sessions. Ordinary people can make perfect sense of the real world and are the experts doing the real work of learning, planning, and implementation
- Rationalization of conflict. As disagreement on certain topics is unavoidable and often legitimate, it is unrealistic to strive for consensus in a community. Rationalization of conflict is about finding the common ground between the arguments as the basis for the community to move forward
- Builds on the notion that people are purposeful, want to learn, and create their own future.

Traditional goal setting and planning methods assume that experts are essential to gather the appropriate data and to craft plans that can be implemented. Traditional planning methods also assume that it is possible to create 5, 10, and 20 year plans based on historical data.

The search conference acknowledges the value of data gathered by experts, but also places greater value and emphasis on the direct knowledge of participants in any system and on their ability to select goals and plan their future.

Changes in the world important into the future

Trends and forces directly affecting our system

Common history of our system

Our current system: what to

keep, drop, create

Desirable future

of our system

Action planning

End of the search conference:

Diffusion to the community

Implementing the plan

Search conference design

The search conference resembles a funnel in its design. It begins with the widest possible perspective, then it narrows down to specific key actions, widening again as the group diffuses and implements its vision to the rest of the community.

The first part of the conference consists of a series of tasks to learn what's happening in the global and more direct environment. This sheds light on how the community is, or could be responding to environmental changes. Next, the community does an appreciative inquiry into the past, exploring its history and heritage, followed by an assessment on the current state of affairs.

Based on the shared information of the environment and community itself, the second part of the conference puts people before the task of developing a vision of their community's most desirable future. The outcome is a series of agreed upon vision statements.

In the last third of the session, participants turn desirable vision statements into achievable goals by anticipating potential constraints and devising strategies to get around them. Finally, action plans and strategies for diffusion and implementation are developed.

Although search conferences are always designed to meet the specific needs of the client system, it generally looks like Figure 2.4.

The Search Conference Is Based On Active, Adaptive Learning and Planning

Unlike the salamander who simply changes color to adapt to the environment, search conference participants actively and creatively plan in a puzzle-solving manner so that they are both learning from and changing the environment as they go. The search process also requires people to do some serious introspection in their effort to both learn about and to get outside of the box of their system.

In short, active adaptation is dependent on an individual's and organization's ability to

- Learn from the environment
- Learn about the system
- Plan a better system

Before returning to the area's second search, let's take a look at why the people in this area came to use the search as a means to change their community.

Why Shapeshift an Old Dutch Settlement?

The Macatawa area is probably one of the healthiest economic climates in the state. New industries are attracted by the area's solid work ethic, abundant resources, and quality of life. For a long time, the Macatawa area has been the home to outstanding companies such as the Prince Corporation, Haworth, Herman Miller, Beverage America, Bil-mar, and Heinz. There is virtually no unemployment in the area with some companies having as many as 90 job openings a week.

A Socio-Ecological Perspective   The vast majority of these large companies are owned by residents of the Macatawa area. Direct local feedback by their neighbors on how their business effects the community, as well as their own direct perception, helps them to face and deal with a wide range of social, economic, and ecological issues as resident citizens and businesses. Keeping pace with the area's long-standing tradition of social responsibility, many of them have reached out in the past to help.

Again, this all sounds as if we were describing heaven, not Holland, Michigan. But with a healthy growing economy comes increasing complexity, many new relationships, and problems more associated with big cities than with small town Michigan. Increasingly, a growing population and changes in its cultural mix created both multiple demands and calls for new responses from the social, economic, political, ecological, and physical infrastructures of the area. Some of these trends as noted in the 2010 Report on the Macatawa area were:

- A projected population increase of around 20% by the year 2000 and 50% by 2010
- A growing Hispanic and Asian population in a conventional Dutch culture
- From having one of the lowest unemployment rates in the state, the area began to experience an increase of gang and drug-related crime. (In 1993 the first police officer fell to the hand of gang violence.)
- Lack of affordable and adequate housing
- Increasing language barriers
- Transportation problems that require comprehensive study and solutions

The need for more regional solutions and the rising concern for the quality of life in the Macatawa area sparked the idea of doing a comprehensive regional planning process to help get a better handle on the future.

Now, for the first time, people in the community realized that there was both the need and opportunity to move beyond piecemeal solutions. Working together through the search conference would enable them to both select and move toward a more desirable future.

Back to the Search Follow Up of 1995

When we left off looking at the sights and sounds of Macatawa's first following up to their search conference, we had just heard an overview of the Environmental Action Team's accomplishments. The next group is one working on personal safety. Here we see Bridgett Staub and Sgt. Gene Koopman reporting out and asking for support on the Personal Safety Action Group that found a place in the more comprehensive Federal Weed and Seed Program. Bridgett is explaining what they've been doing and what's happening right now:

- A task force has been established to combat gang violence, with, among other things, the help of a computer database to track gang related activity.
- Increased street-level law enforcement presence in targeted neighborhoods including additional policing with bike and foot patrols as well as prevention programs for residents.
- Prevention programs are working to strengthen police school relationships, train community members to deal with juvenile crime issues, provide parenting education, and break down the cycle of domestic violence.
- Safe Haven sites have opened at Community Education buildings in the target neighborhoods.

- The Human Services Agency activities are coordinated to maximize availability to residents, often right at the Safe Haven site.
- Childcare workers from within the target neighborhoods are being identified and trained.
- Neighborhood restoration efforts, including repairs and paint blitzes, are helping to overcome deterioration.

Economic development needs are being closely examined in an effort to provide solutions to high poverty levels, unemployment, and underemployment. Sgt. Gene Koopman stated publicly a week later at Weed and Seed's first anniversary, "In spite of the obstacles we still need to overcome, this year has clearly been the best experience in my 20 years with the police force."

The Healthcare Priority Group　The Healthcare Priority Group is breaking ground in its effort to coordinate healthcare and medical services in the entire area. They have been the driving force behind getting the community hospitals of Holland and Zeeland to think in terms of partnership and begin reducing redundant services. Lynn Kotecki explains enthusiastically, "Our next goal is to organize a search conference on health care as a way to get all the right people in the room and knock down the barriers that hinder the breakthrough change we so desperately need."

The Land Use/Transportation Priority Group　Daniel Driesinga explains that the objective to explore future regional land use and regional planning through a geographical information system (GIS) database proved to be so extensive that the Land Use/Transportation Priority Group split off a separate subgroup to just do that. The GIS subgroup has made significant progress. The group is aiming at supplementing the already existing Board of Public Works GIS database with additional electronic data already on file with local governmental units and educational institutions. One of the key benefits of a GIS database at a central data exchange location is the ease with which map and database changes can be made as information changes. Merging several sources of information and data generates numerous GIS uses for: zoning and land use maps; transportation systems; water, sewer, and other utility system maps; election districts; school bus routing and school district maps; tax code maps; environmental contamination site maps; and property ownership maps.

These are but a few of the exciting achievements that the priority action groups presented. The rest of the day was spent on small group and plenary discussions around the feedback from the science fair, evaluating current actions against the changing world, and, in response to that, the setting of possible new task groups. Many new initiatives were generated, most of which could be absorbed by the existing action groups. By the end of the day, the Community Access and Technology Group was added to the list of priority action groups.

A Look at the First Macatawa Search and Why It Was Successful

I can hear some of you readers saying, "Everything went well and they even did a participative follow-up, but how and why did it go so well?" Fair enough question, let's take a look at what makes a search conference live up to its potential.

The purpose of a search conference, again, is to harness the skills needed to understand both complexity and rapid change in our communities and related environment, and then to use those skills to create both a vision of a desirable future and the plans for how to get there.

A Word of Caution   Even if a search produces the very best plans and implementation process imaginable, these can all unwind if participants assume that getting to the desirable future is simply a matter of carrying out those plans in a linear fashion.

Underlying Strengths of the Search   The underlying strength of the search is that it gives the community the ability to constantly probe and scout the environment for new or unforeseen changes, as well as the ability to then create new or enhanced strategies to maintain its course to its desirable future. Both during and after the search, in the diffusion and implementation phase, the community and its plans are not unlike a sailing ship aiming for safe harbor. The changes in course that the ship takes into account for shifting winds and changing currents are analogous to the search community using multiple feedback, learning, and self-referencing loops to stay on course toward its desired future (and in some cases, even alter the desired future). To reach its long-term objective, the search community needs to have people in the crow's nest to spot far away changes and people forward and aft, starboard and leeward, plumbing for changes in depth, and people reviewing the map. They must also maintain their ability to get all hands on deck to adjust their sails when necessary, upgrade navigation equipment, and optimize radio contact. And if the plans no longer fit a rapidly changing environment, the community needs to retain its ability to even redesign the ship.

In non-metaphorical terms, the community needs to retain its ability to continuously monitor the following aspects of the search process:

- Initial reasons and purpose for the search
- Identified boundaries of the system: for example, the group of people who have the knowledge and experience to meet the purpose of the search

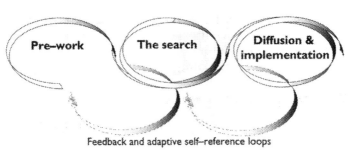

The changes in course that the ship takes into account for shifting winds and changing currents are analogous to the search community using multiple feedback, learning, and self–referencing loops to stay on course toward its desired future.

Figure 2.4 Staying on course requires feedback and learning loops

The search as a heuristic device

Why does a two-and-a-half day event have such a lasting impact on how people think and work? In a search conference people are putting in practice a radically new and different way of working together — quite the opposite of what most of them are used to in their jobs.

Most organizations, institutions, or conferences are, through their expert assumptions, designed to control information, to restrict learning, and inhibit creativity, all for the sake of preserving order and the idea that it is this order that makes the world go round.

The search conference offers an alternative — democratic in its design — it puts the responsibility for control and coordination clearly in the hands of those doing the work. While I am not saying that this is easy, it does have a real advantage. People are making their own decisions, are responsible for their own learning, and are dealing with the challenges of a variety of tasks. As people look to themselves as well as to others for direction, mutual support and respect become indispensable. Seeing the whole picture, to look beyond the usual piecemeal solution coupled with the ability to actually influence the outcome adds real meaning to the work. And, not in the least, it provides opportunity for people to grow and get ahead in life.

Once people have experienced their own authentic power and social creativity in the environment of the search conference (or other democratic designs), the assumed limitations just fall away. From there on, it will be difficult for most to ignore dysfunctional bureaucratic work arrangements.

- Ongoing trends, forces, and changes in the environment
- State of affairs within the system
- Most desirable future state
- Non-bureaucratic nature of the search community

Delivering on Its Promise

Search conferences deliver their promise if proper and careful attention is given to

- The pre-work
- The search itself
- The extended phase of diffusion and implementation

Pre-work: Defining Purpose and Selection of Participants

The hard work of a planning group establishes the front end of the process. Here in Michigan, the planning group was well aware that soon, virtually every public policy would require some form of coordination across and between local independent municipalities. This fact urged the planning group to clearly define an inclusive mission or purpose for the search conference. At the first Macatawa search reception in March 1994, the overhead projector flashed up and read:

> "A gathering of the diverse people of the Macatawa area in a collaborative quest to create a common vision and develop paths to a significant future place."

The reception was called to life to help the selection of participants for the search. Rich vander Broek, a planning group member recalls "It was a grueling selection process, in which our committee took a great deal of effort and time to formulate a slice of our community that was representative of income, age, culture, religion, education, and business community, and so forth. The reception informed community members about the upcoming search event and laid out the participant selection criteria which included the limits to the group size of the search conference, diversity, area-wide representation, and ability to contribute to the process (not just those two days in May). In all, three months later, 63 people showed up at the Big Rapids Search Conference, and Maria Cruz reminded us, 'I was able to see the different roles in the community, for myself I was a student, Hispanic, and a female, so age, diversity, and gender were all there!'"

THE SEARCH ITSELF

In the late afternoon of Tuesday, May 24, 1994, participants started to pour in as they prepared themselves for their first evening session. Freedom from phone calls and other distractions, truly made this search conference a two-and-a-half day social island.

Learning About the Environment

After the orientation, introductions and listing of hopes and expectations for the coming two-and-a-half days, the group begins by brainstorming a long list about the significant changes in the world that they believe will have an impact on the future. The wall is quickly covered with statements and phrases:

- Evolution of new culture
- Emphasis on speed
- Breakdown in family structure
- Medical advances
- Population explosion
- Power of money
- People in ethnic conflicts
- Both spouses working
- Different religious traditions
- Computers and communication
- Aging population
- Environmental resources
- World finance marketshare

Participants are beginning to see their community in a much larger context and when later, the shared ideals come to bear during a heated large group discussion over gender issues, the conference managers know the lid is off the jar and from this point on the Macatawa area people own the search.[5]

The First Evening Closes   The search conference managers, impressed by the boost of energy during the first evening session, hear participants saying as they leave the room, "The gender discussion was great and long overdue!"

The Next Morning and More Exploration of the Environment

The next morning the group advances by exploring the direct effects that changes in their immediate environment have on them. Increased awareness of regional identity, land use pressures, employment-based changes, school to work transitions, competition, cultural shifts, and

---

[5] The real starting point for every search conference manager in a search is the point at which participants take responsibility for their own data and act in a manner that is genuine, open, and public, right up to the point of disagreement.

unfunded mandates are a few of the identified direct stressors on the community. This direct environmental impact scan coupled with last night's analysis of the changes in the world at large helps the group see and understand the correlation between the outside world and the future direction of their community. All these meaningful and sometimes painful deliberations have implications for and bear fruit during the planning of the most desirable future of the Macatawa area.

Learning About the System

Now it is time to move within the boundaries of the system and to appreciate its history and assess its present functioning. Following this, the challenge of creating the most desirable future for the Macatawa area begins.

Our History   The entire group pushes and pulls chairs closer to the center of the room for they know they don't want to miss any of the stories that make this community what it is today. One of the community elders begins:

> "I believe the foundation of who we are today was laid way back when the Dutch Reverend Van Raalte and the first settlers struck down on the shores of Lake Michigan. They had, through their oppression in Europe, strong feelings about religious freedom, hard and honest work, good education, and fine relationship between owners and workers."

Others continue as time and space barriers between people dissolve:

> " . . . the quarreling between the two Dutch settler towns and the fire in downtown Holland in 1871."

> "The building of the civic center some 50 years ago brought people socially together."

> "The evolving of the farming and fruit belt introduced the migrant Hispanic workers to the area, which eventually led to more ethnic diversity."

> "In the late 1950s, 13 individual school systems joined to become a separate district."

> "The massive industry growth over the last 20 years: Haworth and Herman Miller, for example."

> "The Hispanic and Laotian festivals, we are now celebrating many cultures."

"The massive growth on the north side of the city of Holland—malls, the public parks and beaches, railroad, ships, and hotels to attract people to the area."

"The formation of the MACC as a formalized cooperative effort".

"And don't forget: We owe our name to the respected Chief Macatawa from the Ottawa tribe."

"This is a very moving experience. I've learned more about the importance of our own history in this past hour than in the last forty years."

How Are We Doing Today?

As they re-enter the great room after lunch, three flip charts face them labeled, respectively: keep, create, drop. The conference managers can barely keep up the writing as people assess their present state of affairs and call out:

Keep
  "The stop signs at 17th street"
  "Local control over industry"
  "Tax abatement for business attraction"
Drop
  "Duplication of services in township fire and police depart-
  ments"
  "Tax abatements"
  "The 'If you're not Dutch, you're not much' attitude."

The disparities between some municipalities were also noted. Holland has the most people and the highest public service demands, while some townships have dramatically higher average incomes. That is the dubious equation of urban blight evident in so many larger cities—Chicago and Detroit—one that the Macatawa area wants to avoid at all costs.

The next list outperforms the other two by far, it reads:

Create
  "Consistency in land development"
  "An effective area-wide public transportation system"
  "A way to force businesses to address child care for their
  employees"
  "Area wide infrastructure'
  "A computer free-net"
  "Cable programming"
  "A response to increased youth violence and gang issues"

"Enhanced mechanisms for volunteerism in community"
"A Spanish page in the local newspaper"
"More equitable funding among/across municipalities, cities
and townships"

Creating Our Desirable Future

After a recap of the work they have already done, Nancy Cebula, one of
the conference managers, puts the search community on task with this
instruction: "In no more than five statements clearly describe the most
desirable future of the Macatawa area in 1999."

Participants gather in small groups to review the critical data on the
walls, to dream large, be practical, think originally, and present to the
community their view on the most desirable future. After the small
groups report out their future visions, a few people begin cutting and
pasting to integrate approximately 30 statements into a common list. The
entire community is now engaged in a discussion of what statements can
or cannot be merged and which ones definitely stand alone, thus making
absolutely clear what are the different points of view on the future of
Macatawa. When this affinity process is completed, the final list contains
13 different statements. The small groups again retreat to define three criteria to prioritize the list and rank the top five. This helps identify where
the community is willing to put its energy and what it truly wants to
work on for the future. Arduous debate follows when groups report out
their criteria and rankings. The search managers start a process to reach
agreement on what the community will work and action plan for. Debate,
discussion, and finally agreement brings their future to light:

- Ethnic diversity must be celebrated rather than simply tolerated or
  observed.
- Equal access to good quality health care and education must be part
  of the Macatawa region's vision of the future.
- Social services must be well coordinated and aimed at keeping fam-
  ily relationships healthy and preventing further deterioration.
- Crime prevention and law enforcement is a priority.
- Ensuring the future of the natural environment—water, air, and soil.

Finally, the Macatawa search community comes to closure and
announces:

"We, as a community, are committed to improving the quality of life
in the Greater Macatawa Area through creative, cooperative, and
comprehensive work in the following areas:
- Economic development
- Lifelong learning
- Environment
- Personal safety

- Health care
- Residential life
- Land use and transportation
- Social services"

Planning How to Get There

The search conference is as much about strategy as it is about making demo-cratic choices. It aims beyond just being visionary to make the desirable future happen. After people have self-selected the area in which they are most interested in working, Bob Rehm, another of the conference managers, prepares the participants for the hard work of pushing dreams into reality.

He says to the group, "Before we throw ourselves into action planning, I want you to first clearly describe what it is you are going to work for in terms of outcomes. Secondly, I want you to identify at least one major constraint and develop a strategy to either overcome or get around that constraint."

"Let me clarify this point on strategy," says Rehm. "The search confer-ence adopts the strategy of indirect approach as developed in the *Art of War* by Sun Tzu and exemplified in the ancient Chinese game Go. It means the art and science of maneuvering. The message is: 'Do not waste costly resources fighting battles, prevent war.' The action groups are now prepared not to put all their eggs in one basket, but rather develop an array of practical strategies and actions most likely to stand the test of time and uncertainty.

The Plan

The camera of the local cable station zooms in as the land use group reports out on how they will develop a coordinated and comprehensive land use strategy incorporating infrastructure systems inclusive of all the governmental units in the Macatawa area. In great detail, they explain what it is they're going after, who will be involved, who will be responsi-ble, and by when. The community has some questions for clarification and provides feedback. They all applaud the fruits of intense and hard work. The camera swings on to the next group.

BACK TO THE WORLD

"The Macatawa Area Coordinating Council is willing to provide this search community all the support and resources that we have at our dis-posal; we are not here to receive the results of this conference, they are yours," says Sue Higgins, conference participant and director of MACC. She continues her commentary by saying, "It is the community's respon-sibility to control and coordinate their own work as they set out to attain their future goals. As a bottoms-up support system the MACC has avoided the trap of creating another bureaucracy. Volunteers from each

Action Priority Group form a coordinating group. They will act as a clearing house, to ease the access to the different action groups, to disperse information on progress, to respond to specific needs, et cetera."

Suddenly we are at the end of the first search conference. One participant sums it up well as he speaks into the camera: "It gave me great joy to be part of this because I've been involved with so many organizations and committees that have no idea and don't even care about what is going on in the community—they have no compassion and sensitivity. I'm proud to have been part of this search conference."

SOME CLOSING THOUGHTS ON THE SEARCH AND DIRECT DEMOCRACY

In stark contrast to how most of our organizations and political institutions are operating, the Macatawa search community, even with its ups and downs, continues to function as an open, adaptive system, which has a clear understanding that issues are not resolved in isolation. They have truly become champions and catalysts for change, bringing numerous parties together to help them shift gears as soon as the big picture emerges for them. Through their own search experience, action group members have modeled for the rest of the community that all people are natural learners, and demonstrated the power of collective learning and planning.

While many in this nation cry out that they have been disempowered by their government or that democracy is a poor way to make decisions, the people in the Macatawa area are, perhaps without even being aware of it, mocking the naysayers by successfully practicing direct participative democracy while working to create their most desirable future.

THE PARTICIPATIVE DESIGN APPROACH

Participative design enables organizations to redesign themselves fast and cost effectively through the involvement of the people whose work is changing. The vehicle to do the redesign is called the *participative design workshop* (PDW). With clearly understood design principles and simple tools to analyze their situation, natural work groups can redesign themselves in three days. An entire organization should not take longer than a few weeks. The outcome is a highly flexible, adaptive organization, structured around self-managed groups, with the capacity to learn continuously.

Participative Design Makes Common Sense

Most work redesign strategies today impose expert solutions on the organization and often take months just to do the data gathering and diagnostics. A select team of internal and external experts extract data, detailing every measure of input, output, business processes, the reporting relationships, and social conditions.

Of course, the people who already know all that are the people that work there! Moreover, they already have ideas, and in many cases strong views, as to how their work sections can be changed for the betterment of themselves, their peers, and the enterprise as a whole. By pooling their initiatives for change, they themselves can redesign their workplace. Having people participate in the design of their own work establishes that every person, from the president to the front-line employee, can be a researcher, learner, teacher, and resource.

A clear, conceptual understanding of the basic structure of work and what motivates people to put their best foot forward is all you need for this do-it-yourself work redesign method.

What Motivates People to Do Excellent Work?

More than 30 years of social science research on what motivates people in their work has identified a number of important requirements for productive activity. When work conditions are favorable and meet these requirements, productivity, quality, and people's well-being soar. Involving both tasks and social climate, the core requirements are:

1. *Adequate elbow room for decision making.* The sense that people can influence their own work and that, with the exception of specific circumstances, they don't have to ask permission for everything. People need enough elbow room to feel empowered but not so much that they do not know what to do.

2. *Opportunity to learn continually on the job.* Such learning is possible when people can set goals that are reasonable challenges for them and get timely feedback on results.

3. *An optimum level of variety.* Through the avoidance of boredom and fatigue, people can gain the best advantages from settling into a satisfying and effective rhythm of work.

4. *Mutual support and respect.* Conditions where people can and do get help and respect from their co-workers.

5. *Meaningfulness.* A sense of one's own work contributing meaningfully to society. Also, to have knowledge of the whole product or service. Many jobs lack meaningfulness, because workers see only such a small part of the final product that meaning is denied to them.

6. *A desirable future.* Put simply, not a dead-end job, but one with a career path which will allow personal growth and increase in skills.

The Solution Lies in the Structure of Work

The obvious question is: "How can we meet today's business objectives and integrate the core requirements for productive activity into our work setting?" The answer is the participative design approach. Radically different from any other (re)design methods, participative design traces problems around productivity, quality, and motivation straight to the core of organizational structure. It distinguishes two design principles which have far-reaching consequences as to:

- How coherent and focused the organization is
- How adaptive and flexible the organization is to demands and opportunities from its environment
- How challenged and motivated people are to do excellent work and help the organization to grow its business

Design Principle One (DP One): Redundancy of Parts

For organizations to respond adequately to market demand and changes in the environment, they need to behave flexibly and adaptively. This is only possible by building in a degree of redundancy. The critical feature of DP One structures is that responsibility for coordination and control is located at least one level above where the work is done. This enables companies to treat workers as if they were redundant of replaceable parts. An example is the traditional assembly line, where a worker is limited to a segmented piece of work, and can be easily replaced by another worker (replaceable part) who needs little, if any, training to do the simple tasks. Through its focus on tasks, the traditional organization is made up of narrowly skilled, replaced people whose work is closely controlled and coordinated by supervisors one step above the work. By the nature of its structure, a DP One organization defeats some or all of the core requirement for productive activity.

Design Principle Two (DP Two): Redundancy of Functions

By adding extra functions to each operating part, employees broaden their roles outside of sheer job classifications. Being skilled in a wide variety of social and technical tasks, it is now much easier to respond adequately and flexibly to demand placed on the system. So, in contrast to DP One, each person can perform multiple functions and tasks. An example is the self-managing group in which people learn many functions that can be applied when needed.

The critical feature of DP Two is that responsibility for coordination and control of the work is located exactly where it is done.

DP Two structure work groups are typically responsible for:

- Client satisfaction, quality, and productivity measures
- Development and management of budgets
- Scheduling of work
- Design of work process and flow
- Layout of workplace
- Hiring decisions
- Peer reviews

What Happens in a Typical Participative Design Workshop?

A participative design workshop generally follows this sequence and includes the following elements:

Assessment

- Briefing one: A short presentation of design principle one, the bureaucratic organization and its inverse relationship to the six criteria for productive work. Explanation for completing the six criteria matrix and the skills matrix.
- Groups complete the matrices for the six criteria and the skills matrix.
- Report and analysis.

Design

- Briefing two: An introduction to design principle two, the democratic and self-managing organization and its relation to the six criteria and skills.
- Groups chart out their current process or work flow. Next, they draw up the formal organizational chart with its reporting relationships. With the self-managing model of DP Two in mind, the groups will then redesign their organizational structure.
- Interim reports.

Implementation

- Briefing three: A list of other critical tasks to help groups make their designs work. This list includes:
  A comprehensive set of measurable goals (quality, quantity, and social)
  Training requirements
  Internal coordination and external relations (meeting management, mechanisms to coordinate and control work, equipment, and resources)

Creating a career path on payment for proven skills and skill blocks
Revisit the six criteria matrix to explain how the new design will
improve the scores.

- Complete the design: The groups make final changes/refinements
to their design and get as far with practical tasks as they can. It's
important to have a plan to continue working on tasks that may
need management negotiation and/or more involvement of others.
- Final reports: The presentation of final reports will require the presence of management depending on how the new design affects
resource needs, challenges, and existing goals.

EXAMPLES OF PARTICIPATIVE DESIGN IN ORGANIZATIONS

Syncrud Canada

An oil company in Alberta, Canada has used the participative design
approach for the past five years. During that time, workforce productivity
has increased more than 55%. Their cost per barrel of oil has dropped from
Can$17.50 to Can$14. With no change in capital equipment, production
output has increased from 60 to 74 million barrels of oil per year.

Champion International

At Champion International, one of the paper mills used participative
design to restructure itself and combined 11 departments into 4 indepen-
dently operating business systems. Each now operates as its own profit/
loss center.

Consulting Firm

In a large international consulting firm, a subgroup that has responsibility for the firm's internal training and development restructured their
work using a participative design workshop. With upfront guarantees for
job security and pay, the group reordered its fragmented structure into an
integrated whole. They eliminated supervisory structure and designed a
seamless and functionally integrated workgroup. Within this workgroup,
they had clear goals, newly designed career opportunities, and a clear
notion that anybody's business is everyone's business.

State Hospital School

In Iowa, the State Hospital School used a participative design workshop
as the means to prepare their managers for complying with new Federal
regulations, to deal with past layoffs and to meet the increasing demands

that the school continuously improve the effectiveness of their outpatient and community services. In their design toward self-management they eliminated two decision making layers and created in its place a leadership group that would charter initiatives and/or projects by pulling together the appropriate players from the frontline to the back office. Their intention is to involve the rest of the organization in the redesign of their own work.

Motorola

At Motorola, the newly formed Management Center (a part of Motorola University) had the challenge of coordinating a group of people to run their respective management institutes, providing educational support for the China and India markets, and designing education products. Motorola also wanted this group to stay on the cutting edge of both management and leadership theory and practice. After an initial strategic planning search process, they used the participative design approach to redesign their work. The strategic search gave them a clearer sense of their desired goals or end points and the pressing urgencies of their direct work environment. With that strategic work as a backdrop, their ensuing design eliminated functional segmentation and produced a structure of work that makes better use of their collective resources and talents and enabled people to go beyond their former job descriptions.

CLOSING THOUGHT

Perhaps the most important gain that participative design brings is that the process of learning becomes as important as the final organizational solution. Said differently: Instead of constantly trying to adapt to change, participative design changes the organization to being adaptive.

Author's note: A special note of thanks to Bob Rehm and Nancy Cebula who were my co-conspirators at the 1994 Macatawa search, and to Fred and Merrelyn Emery whose long and arduous work and research accounts for much of the success of the Macatawa search.

 Frank Heckman is one of the leaders in the search conference and participative design methods in the U.S. He has researched ways to integrate flow into the design of work in organizations. Heckman and his network partners have successfully applied these methodologies in a variety of environments/communities, corporations, state and federal government agencies, educational

institutions, and regional groups in both the U.S. and in Europe. He has a degree in sports and education from the Hogeschool in Amsterdam, and an M.A. in Organizational Development from Loyola University in Chicago. E-mail: crow@MHTC.NET

REFERENCES

Ackoff, R., and Emery, F. E. *On Purposeful Systems.* London: Tavistock Publications, 1972.

Chance, M. R. A. *Social Fabrics of the Mind.* Birmingham, United Kingdom: Social Systems Institutes, 1988.

Csikszentmihalyi, M. *Creativity.* New York: HarperCollins Publishers, 1996.

Csikszentmihalyi, M. *The Evolving Self.* New York: HarperCollins Publishers, 1993.

Csikszentmihalyi, M. *Flow, the Psychology of Optimal Experience.* New York: Harper & Row, 1990.

Ehin, C. "The Quest for Empowering Organizations: Some Lessons from Our Foraging Past." *Organization Science.* Vol. 6, No. 5, 1996.

Emery, F. E. *Systems Thinking, Vol. I & II.* Harmondworth, England: Penguin Books, 1981.

Emery, F. E., and Thorsrud, E. *Democracy at Work; The Report of the Norwegian Industrial Democracy Program.* Leiden, The Netherlands: Martinus Nijhof, 1976.

Emery, F. E., and Trist, E. L. "The Causal Texture of Organizational Environments." *Human Relations,* 1976.

Emery, M., ed. *Participative Design for Participative Democracy.* Canberra, Australia: Australian National University, 1993.

Emery, M. "Searching for New Directions, in New Ways." *New Times.* Canberra, Australia: Australian National University, 1982.

Heckman, F. H. F. "A New Method for Achieving Community Excellence." *The Journal for Quality and Participation,* December 1995.

Heckman, F. H. F. "The Participative Design Approach." *The Journal for Quality and Participation,* March 1996.

Kaufman, S. *At Home in the Universe.* New York: Oxford University Press, 1995.

Power, M. "Back to the Future: A Commentary on *The Quest for Empowering Organizations.*" *Organization Science.* Vol. 6, No. 6, 1995

Power, M. *The Egalitarians, Human and Chimpanzee.* Cambridge: Cambridge University Press, 1991.

Suzuki, D., and Knudson, P. *Wisdom of the Elders.* New York: Bantam Books, 1993.

Turnbull, C. M. *The Forest People.* New York: Simon & Schuster, 1962.

Waldrop, M. M. *Complexity, The Emerging Science at the Edge of Chaos and Order.* New York: Simon & Schuster, 1992.

EDITOR'S NOTE:

At first thought, the idea that in Ireland, one could find a process that stimulates innovation, cooperative learning, and change might seem a bit far-fetched. The popular view of Ireland seems to be nostalgia for a golden past, a love for its wonderful songs and poets, or fright at the seemingly cruel violence that takes away from the first two views.

Think again. Tom Lyons has constructed and field tested a highly rational and pragmatic method for achieving effective, large-scale change. A special word is needed here so the reader will appreciate that this large scale change does not mean several hundred or several thousand people in one organization. *Shared Learning,* Mr. Lyons' approach to change, has facilitated effective simultaneous change processes in one case for twelve communities (125,000) people and in another case for ten different private and public organizations (30,000 employees). This is large-scale change of a quantum scale.

A change process which can successfully facilitate a process wherein ten organizations from the North and South of Ireland work together to introduce employee participation in one case and bring together twelve economically depressed communities to develop plans simultaneously to improve the economic viability of their communities and to learn from each other in another case is not just a strong process, it is a robust process.

Success at facilitating large-scale change that stimulates innovation, cooperative learning and change is laudable: Achieving it in very difficult and tension filled environments has proven to me that it is perhaps the most robust and adaptable change process yet developed. Ireland and the European Union may be the first beneficiaries of its effectiveness and adaptability but I expect that before we all see the end of the next decade, 2010, it will have revolutionized change and modernization processes throughout the developed and developing world.

Chapter 3

Shared Learning

Tom Lyons, The Irish Productivity Centre

In an age filled with rapid political, social, and technical change, the time-honored approaches to working, managing, and leading seem to be as out of place as a steam locomotive and its attendant crafts would be at a 1990s industrial trade show. No amount or speed of change has relieved us of the need for effectiveness and rigor in the processes and methods we use to facilitate the forming and reforming of our enterprises or our work.

Shared Learning is a structured method for developing and implementing specific, system-wide change within timeframe and resource limits set by the participants. Its effectiveness and rigor have been proved out under the harshest of conditions and within a variety of difficult settings.

After more than a decade of evolution and success in its application it can now be said that in Shared Learning, we have a very robust process which can support effective change and transformation in a wide variety of whole systems and settings.

Shared Learning can and has facilitated effective change and transformation in:

- Single organizations (for profit and not-for-profit) which had decided that the union and management needed to find new ways of working together for mutual benefit.
- A network of ten different public and private enterprises in the North and South of Ireland which set out simultaneously to improve their performance through the introduction of critical changes based on a variety of employee participation processes.
- Twelve communities on the island of Ireland, not including Northern Ireland, all of which wanted to substantially advance their local economic development capacity and success in a coherent and integrated manner.
- Organizations which desired to improve performance and decision making within multiple divisions or with multiple unions.

A MULTI-ORGANIZATIONAL SHARED LEARNING PROCESS

The rigor of Shared Learning at this stage of its evolution is demonstrated by the following project results (achieved within a strict March 1985/ March 1987 project timeframe). Within ten organizations (30,000 employees) during a two-year program, some 30 change initiatives were introduced and barriers to change were removed. The sample initiatives shown are not in any order of priority, occurrence, or importance.

Each initiative, however, was concerned with a sensitive issue within the particular organization in which it was introduced. The initiatives included:

• The introduction of a training and development policy and job appraisal scheme
• The establishment of agreed principles for the development of a draft joint technology agreement
• The design, processing, and feedback of a company-wide attitude survey
• The development and commencement of a five-year flexibility training program
• The introduction and establishment of cross-department project team working
• The introduction of customer service teams on a pilot basis
• The achievement of 100% employee adherence to health care regulations on hearing protection
• The introduction of job preservation/creation—an intrapreneurship initiative

---

Participating Organizations in the Multi-Organizational Process

Telecom Eireann (telecommunications)	Northern Ireland Electricity Service (electricity generation and distribution)
Irish Gas (natural gas sales & distribution)	Northern Ireland Housing Executive (public sector housing; building & maintenance)
National Physical Planning Research Institute (research)	Ulster Museum (preservation & display of antiquities)
Waterford Crystal (crystal glass manufacturers)	Rothmans (NI) Ltd. (cigarette manufacturers: had to leave mid-project)
Virginia Milk Products (milk processing)	Sir Richard Arkwright (textiles— spinning)
Ten independent organizations employing *30,000* people	

THE INTEGRATED RURAL DEVELOPMENT PROJECT (TIMEFRAME: OCT. 4, 1988–OCT. 5, 1990)

Although many of the Integrated Rural Development projects, as of October, 1990, were still in the early stages, those reported on had led to the creation of 225 full-time jobs. These projects further targeted a potential employment of 600 full-time jobs, 687 part-time jobs, and 1,500 short-term seasonal jobs. Altogether, this amounted to about 5% of the working population of the areas.

Many of the projects undertaken generated additional or supplementary incomes for people. Within the pilot phase, additional income amounted to $1,000,000 per annum.

The potential income for projects underway amounts to $8,700,000 per annum. (This figure leaves out the potential results of quite a large number of projects where the impact was not quantified.) From the perspective of individuals, this means that $8.7 million provides $8,750 per capita for 980 people. For people in the pilot areas such as small farmers, fishermen, or others with mainly seasonal or part-time employment and relatively low incomes, such sums could be sufficient to make the difference between involuntary emigration and reasonably acceptable living standards for perhaps $2^1/_2$ to 4% of the working population.

We are now achieving similar results in a number of private, company stand-alone applications and with organizations dealing with multiple union partners within the same multi-site organization.

The Shared Learning process is not, of course, the miraculous result of a single planning and design session. The maturity and rigor it has now is based upon more than a decade's work with input from hundreds of participants, as well as the dedication and insight of colleagues and advisors from Ireland, the UK, the European Union, North America, and Scandinavia.

THE EVOLUTION OF SHARED LEARNING

An understanding of our learning path about how to both speed up and enhance the effectiveness of organizational transformation will help you, I believe, understand that with this process, you can now approach a whole system change with a great deal more confidence.

As often as not our learning comes from the (sometimes simultaneous) discovery that

- What seems to be a very complex situation or problem has a relatively simple answer.
- What seemed to be very simple and straightforward at the beginning, turns out to need a fairly complex approach.

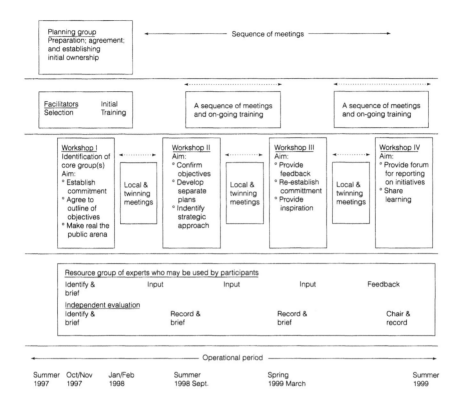

Figure 3.1 The design of a typical Shared Learning process

Let's consider some examples, and on the way you'll see the how, what, and why of this approach to change called Shared Learning, and why it works and sticks.

For more generations than most could remember, when an organization, community, or society discovered a problem that needed changing, the approach was to suggest, "Let's try a number of different approaches on a small scale, then select the best one and tell everyone to copy that one!"

Too often, much too often, this type of pilot or model project is not only thought to be a safe and less costly way to solve a problem or to introduce change but we convince ourselves as well that surely it will apply to the whole system. The answer is then so obvious that all anyone needs to do is to copy the model and apply it everywhere in the same manner and achieve the same results.

"I'll learn you"

This reminds me of my first steps in my journey to understanding something of learning and effective change. My first lesson was in my grandmother's kitchen. Although she loved me dearly, I was quite clear on the point that it was still wise to keep the large country kitchen table between the two of us when my actions led her to say, "If I get close to you young man, I'll learn you." Her intentions were kindly, to be sure, but her intended method of learning me her right way was one that I resisted. At the very least, I wanted to have some say in learning what was best for me. And even then, I knew from hand-me-down trousers and sweaters that clearly, one size doesn't fit all.

Over the years, my grandmother's unintended lesson reminded me that there is seldom one right way and that having someone "learn you" would usually produce nothing other than a great deal of resistance or avoidance.

Much later, in the 1970s, while working with my colleagues, mentors, and the late Professor Keith Thurley (London School of Economics) and Dr. Hans Wirdenius of F. A. Radet on *The Future Role and Development of Supervision in the UK, Sweden, and Ireland,* my kitchen table-based knowledge came into sharp focus.

The Future Role and Development of Supervision in the United Kingdom, Sweden, and Ireland Initiative

This initiative called for sending teams of international experts in supervision into seven different types of factories with parent firms from the US, Germany, France, Sweden, Japan, and Ireland to carry out a diagnosis of existing supervisory practices in one week.

During this brief study, it became clear that

- Standardized recommendations or prescriptions would just not do the job—recommendations tailor made for each firm would be required.
- Traditional training solutions for individuals would not do the job—there was a need to make overall organizational changes.
- There was a need to redesign the supervisory role and a general upgrading of the role.
- Decisions should be decentralized to give supervisory management systems greater control and autonomy.
- A technical improvement role would have to be developed for supervisors.
- A systematic analysis of the supervisory role in each company was needed as the basis for radical restructuring of the role and that such a restructuring could only take place within an overall change process.

One case within this initiative, in particular, demonstrated to me the value of *shared* learning. A diagnosing group dominated by French experts visited a German owned and managed firm doing business in Ireland. The French dominated team gave the German manager a very frank assessment and a radical set of recommendations to overcome *his* above-average absenteeism and labor turnover in the face of the then 17% unemployment in the community. Three years later, this German chief executive came back to the organizers of the initiative and told us that the "French intervention" was the most valuable lesson he had ever received in his business experience. Later, after the initiative had concluded, while we were sharing experiences about the design of training programs for mid-level personnel (including supervisors), my memory of the role of the kitchen table led us to see that:

"It's not all about trainers training, it's more about learners learning."

Who Owns the Change or Learning?

My grandmother's failure to learn me whatever she had in mind from the other side of the table stood out for me as an ownership issue. Her learn me intention was to pass to me some understanding of a particular danger into which she was determined I should not fall. The kindly intent was to separate danger and learning. The result, of course, was that I could only apply her learning as if it were a narrowly designed rule—it did me little good in situations not covered by her learning.

My additional learning from this line of thought and experience was that even though it might be impossible to include everyone in the system in a single learning event or experience, you should include as many people as is possible who are, either formally or informally, leaders or people with respected influence.

The danger of leaving out relevant decision makers needs to be faced during the design stage. The key is to involve a large enough and complete enough (representative) slice of the total system to avoid the risk of seeing the initiative sidelined or bypassed later as a real means of transforming the system.

The Role of Experts

If it's about learners learning, and we know that learners closely watch how feet move relative to lips, then the use of experts during learning has to be consistent with the concept of learners learning. It is not the need for experts that is at issue; this need is nearly always clear. The issue is the role and profile of experts within the learning, problem solving, or innovation process. An expert may have a key role, but in many cases should not have high visibility or authority within the process. The focus on the needs of learners learning led us to pay careful attention to being consistent with that principle throughout any learning or change process, lest we fall back in to the *we'll learn you* mode of training.

In a current case in the computer industry, the profile of the Shared Learning facilitator's role is low so as not to lessen the importance/legitimacy of members of the joint steering group for partnership (labor and management). All preparatory work for the partnership has been off-site, so as to not take away from the profile of the on-site joint steering group.

WHICH IS MORE EFFECTIVE: LEARNING WITH FOLKS JUST LIKE US, OR LEARNING WITH STRANGERS?

During a participative learning event, *The Future Role and Development of Supervision in the UK, Sweden, and Ireland*, we observed how the sharing of distinctly different aspirations and experiences, had created a synergy between participants. Their dissimilarities, instead of hindering the learning process, had in fact enhanced their ability to focus on processes and the organization of such processes (the governance or political aspects of organization) rather than their ability to talk past each other by focusing on the specifics of their different companies and countries.

While this experience taught us much about how learners can better learn together, it also demonstrated to us that while one event or one week led to some significant learning, it was not enough contact time between groups to lead to significant impact in each workplace.

A change in career focus from researching and restructuring supervisory roles to designing and supporting employee involvement and participative change processes gave me the opportunity to examine how these actual experiences might be applied to helping organizations design and implement large-scale change processes. I wondered if the insight of *It's about learners learning* and the learning which flowed from that could

- Make the learning about and implementation of partnerships for change processes more effective.
- Hasten both the dissemination of knowledge about participative processes and the diffusion of effective employee involvement processes.

This inclination, coupled with the knowledge that the European Economic Community (now the European Union) would be funding pilot application projects on participative change, led me to opt for taking on several rigorously designed multi-organization change projects from the mid to late 1980s and onwards with the determination that they would pilot a Shared Learning process which focused on learners learning and not just another one right way to introduce workplace partnership into all organizations or systems.

WHAT HAVE WE LEARNED TO DATE?

In a nutshell, both the multi-site projects and single-site projects taught us that effective organizational change had more to do with *POLITICS* than it did with attitudes and that the *HOW* to mobilize a number of people to bring about the desired change is equally important to *WHAT*, or the objective of the change. By *POLITICS* I mean:

- Who participates in the change or learning process
- What rules are applied to interactions and decision making
- What relationships are implemented

Inside a workplace, or within a community of organizations learning together, it's not just an enhanced product *at the right price and at high quality* that determines success. The quality of the change process itself is judged by:

- Who participates in the process
- What rules are applied to it
- What relationships are implemented

Critical Design Features of Shared Learning

Almost 12 years of practical experience with Shared Learning have taught me and my colleagues much about what works well and which design features are indispensable to an effective organizational learning process. The points below sum up these design and conceptual features. In the following sections, each will be further explained and illustrated with examples from successful applications of Shared Learning.

1. Joint ownership of the change process must be acknowledged from the onset. This is demonstrated through the establishment of core groups of people (drawn from the distinct stakeholders in the change process) who are capable of influencing all levels of the organization and will serve as the process leaders of the change process.

2. As early as possible and in every situation a formal joint statement (signed by the principle participants) about why and how the participants will work together toward a jointly chosen future must be developed and communicated widely. This will facilitate mobilizing the necessary numbers of people needed to become active in the development of solutions to problems and means to reach jointly held goals.

3. Agree upon a starting and ending date and transition phases, and identify and allocate personnel, as well as budget on that basis.

4. Make the discomfort of travelling for crucial knowledge an important part of the learning design. Participants must demonstrate their commitment to the process and goals by physically and mentally travelling some distance to gain and share knowledge. Off-site meetings mean that all parties are working together on neutral turf. Additional statements about the learning process and its goals, in conjunction with the formal joint statement, demonstrate that participants have moved away (travelled) from traditional positions toward a different future.

5. Consciously create a number of public arenas within each working change process.

6. Core groups are paired with unlike core groups (between whole system public arena meetings) to share experiences and learnings so as to enhance overall learning and working toward developing solutions to problems and/or establishing means to achieve goals.

7. *Enough trust,* as distinct from absolute trust, must be maintained between the participants—the formal joint statement is the first demonstration of *enough trust.* Trust is earned as people work together toward agreed-upon ends. It can be built and rebuilt (as needed) as people work within the agreed-upon process parameters—the rules of the game.

8. High-profile process leadership and interaction between key individuals of the joint steering group is critical for success.

9. The *HOW* of diffusing results, decisions, and implementation should be an integral part of the process of change and should be carried out at the earliest possible time.

10. An estimate of what outcomes or rewards will accrue to the different stakeholders in the overall change program should be made explicit within the identifiable cycles of feedback built into the actual change process.

JOINT OWNERSHIP OF THE CHANGE PROCESS MUST BE ACKNOWLEDGED FROM THE ONSET

A Shared Learning change process may begin with the insight, vision, or request of a chief executive, a labor union, a group of managers within a single organization, a joint decision by some combination of those just mentioned, a government initiative, or from a number of organizations interested in implementing significant change to improve their economic sector or community. Regardless of where the impetus for change begins, it is imperative that everyone (all groups and individuals with interests in the outcome) impacted by the project feels that they have joint ownership of both the problem and the solution. Since it is not practical for all those who might be impacted by the project to participate in the process, legitimate representatives of the different interests and interested groups must be selected to work together toward solving the identified problem or finding the means to achieve the common goal.

The people who represent the key interest groups within the organization, or between organizations, must be seen as being capable of identifying the most sensitive issues, offering workable solutions to the problem or means to achieving the goals of the project and working together to carry out the change process.

Identifying both the key interest groups and who within them is capable of exercising legitimate influence throughout all levels of the organization is an essential first step toward a successful Shared Learning process. These groups, and the people within them selected as influential and capable individuals, make up the decision making and ownership foundation for the process. Once identified, they are grouped into what we refer to as *core groups*.

Using position titles as starting points for identifying individuals with influence to work on the project is just that, a starting point. In gathering together a vertical slice, you look for someone from middle management and the shop floor who is seen by others as being both capable, influential, and trustworthy. In short, individuals with formal (title) and informal (effective) influence and ability are sought out as key participants in the joint process. Those who have seen important projects sidelined or derailed because one or two key informal leaders have not bought into the project, will, I am sure, appreciate the importance of including as many of those with effective influence and ability in the improvement or change process planning and design.

Core Groups

A core group is most often made up of a vertical slice of the organization or system where change has been proposed:

- In a single-site business, the core group typically has a top-level person, one level down from the chief executive, and a faction of people representing different interest groups from senior management, middle level, to shop floor and, as necessary, based upon white collar and blue collar union allegiances.
- If a multi-site organization is undertaking a Shared Learning process, the core groups for the whole process are made up of core

groups representing each of the sites and possibly a core group from the headquarters operation.

- In a multi-organizational Shared Learning process core group, whose members are selected as in the examples above, members take on leadership roles within their own organizations in pursuit of the jointly identified initiatives within their organization. In this type of process, individuals are nominated by their different interest groups because of their recognized ability to influence their own workplace and their potential to introduce change.
- In a single or multi-community *Shared Learning* process, each core group consists of eight to ten individuals, reflecting a range of backgrounds, experience, and competencies.

Core group members (volunteer activists) also have to have a strong commitment to area improvement and a willingness to make the effort necessary to bring about such development.

A Special Note about Single-Site, Non-Unionized Firms

Some, at this point, may be thinking that core groups do not make sense in single-site organizations without unions—think again. Most people experience their organization as their work group or perhaps their functional department. The people in accounting, assembly, sales, customer services, marketing, et cetera all work and live in the world of their department's functional area of expertise and responsibility. To make matters worse, the folks in accounts receivable work and live in a world that seems quite different from accounts payable. The value of using core groups drawn from different functional groups should now be clearer. As I discuss other critical aspects of Shared Learning, keep the notion that we each work and live in somewhat separate worlds in mind and it should help you see the value of using the Shared Learning process in a non-unionized, single-site firm.

The challenge to organizations is to send out the first team, the competent ones, the ones that are not easily put forward as representatives, but the ones who, in fact, influence decision making. That is critical— absolutely critical—to the success of any Shared Learning initiative. These are the people who become the leading edge and human face of the change process on the ground and take responsibility for the operation of pilot programs or diffusion within their own areas. Members of these core groups should be seen as clearly able people with independent judgement. Individuals seen by others as yes men or perennial naysayers are not good candidates for core groups, regardless of their formal position.

At the heart of the first Shared Learning process was a network of ten separate organizations. The creation of this network of mixed organizations, each of them intent on introducing change simultaneously, was crucial to success of the project. The data from this first application suggested that it was a robust design and that it was very effective in mobilizing participants toward creating new approaches to solving problems. The participative nature of the design, along with other key elements such as networking between companies and the joint decision to achieve results within set time and budget limits, proved most effective in creating a sense of ownership within an organization for its change process.

Mobilizing for Organization-Wide or System-Wide Action

During the Shared Learning process devoted to rural economic development, the depth and breadth of how core groups can mobilize people for action and change was clearly demonstrated. Core groups organized others to work with them.

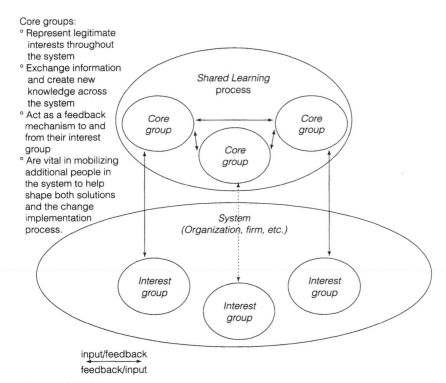

Figure 3.2 Core Groups Gather Up and Diffuse Information

Collectively, over the twelve areas, core groups directly worked with over 70 subgroups. Subgroups were of two basic types: groups with a sectoral (or project focus) and groups with a focus on specific geographical districts. Once internal or local ownership is established, it is hugely valuable establishing both commitment to and momentum for the process and diffusion of its outputs.

A FORMAL JOINT STATEMENT ABOUT THE FUTURE SHOULD BE DEVELOPED AND COMMUNICATED WIDELY

Agreement on process legitimacy must come early and is essential to creating a critical mass for change out of the first mobilization of people for that change. An enabling statement or process charter facilitates a sense of ownership and commitment and mobilizes the numbers of people needed to develop solutions to problems and/or means to reach jointly held goals. In the best examples, a formal statement should outline the scope, intent, and nature of the change program and be distributed widely by the key participants to groups who will be involved in or affected by the change process.

Why Are Such Statements Useful?

Progress toward a breakthrough to achieving a critical mass of people and action for change is about permanently adjusting the *power paradigm* within the organization, or at least adjusting it for the negotiated time period of the change program. Where there is a history of distrust or skepticism, the perception of *process legitimacy* is of paramount importance. Even though workplace change processes may not closely resemble peace talks between nations, to understand the importance of process legitimacy, one need only recall the weeks of discussions between the U.S. and the Vietnamese over the shape of the peace conference table, who would enter the room when, and where they would sit in relation to each party to the negotiations. The most successful Shared Learning initiatives have been those whose joint statements represented the intensity of participation and extent of foreseen mobilization of resources and people for change.

Well-constructed joint statements do not specify how the joint project will proceed on day-to-day issues, nor do they advocate co-management or co-representation as a means to alter established collective bargaining agreements or personnel systems in non-union firms. They should, however, provide for the possibility of working in partnership to cope proactively with ongoing or future change projects or challenges to the organization. From a well-constructed enabling statement, all parties should be able to discern a set of change program operating principles, the spirit of the joint intent, and key practices/behaviors by those participating in the process. Participants should be encouraged to view the enabling statement as a *permanent draft statement* in terms of specifics (not principles). This will allow participants to update or amend the joint statement in light of actual working experience.

Over the years, these consensus building joint statements have had titles such as:

- Joint Statement on Participation
- Enabling Statement (toward bringing about a radical change in shopfloor relationships)
- Compact on Constructive Participation and Requisite Arrangements
- Context for Integrated Rural Development

AGREE UPON A STARTING AND ENDING DATE, TRANSITION PHASES, AND IDENTIFY AND ALLOCATE PERSONNEL, AS WELL AS BUDGET ON THAT BASIS

Setting limits to project work (and project group activity) facilitates rather than hinders the emergence of genuinely collaborative arrangements in the pursuit of substantively important goals. Demonstrating process rigor and discipline in times of scarce resources and mounting pressures for results helps assure support for the process and adds to the probability of its success. Jointly set limits have one additional advantage: It is much easier to get the chief executive of a firm, a union, a town, or a unit of government to commit a set amount of time and funds for a project. In short, people will commit because they are not signing up for life and because the process recognizes where participation stops and negotiation begins. Executives may well realize that change is permanent, but establishing limits around specific changes assures everyone that something will actually get done—on time and within budget.

Shared Learning supports the creation of an event culture. By this I mean it is a problem-led participation process, based upon an agreement by all parties concerned to adopt the project disciplines, parameters, and decision-making process for a specific setting and a fixed timeframe only. This restriction actually frees participants to enter fully into collaboration without having to contract to a new way of forever working together in advance of any actual experience. The strength and acceptability of the process once established, is best demonstrated by the fact that new change initiatives are still being introduced today (years after the end of the formal Shared Learning change process). Experience, in short, creates *enough trust* to take on new initiatives based upon explicit expectations surrounding time, resources, and consistent collaborative decision making processes.

Not a Day Longer and Not a Penny More

In the largest initiative undertaken to date (the Integrated Rural Development pilot project for Europe), we agreed to and adhered to a two-year time limit and a budget of IR£1.5 million to establish an effective process within twelve subregional areas with 125,000 total residents. Our slogan "not a day longer and not a penny more" proved very useful and helped put in place a business-like set of approaches that delivered impressive results. Likewise, in other situations, resource allocations dedicated to achieving results such as promulgation, transition, and diffusion are totally appropriate—nothing inappropriate is likely to occur simply because participants are under pressure to achieve results.

When significant financial resources are needed to support public sector culture change, they will be assembled under the authority of the appropriate governmental body. The government and participants will begin the change proposals designed to help the organization reach and maintain standards of international competitiveness on a growing range of core business activities.

MAKE THE DISCOMFORT OF TRAVELLING FOR CRUCIAL KNOWLEDGE AN IMPORTANT PART OF THE LEARNING DESIGN

Mobilizing numbers of people for joint problem solving needs to be seen and treated as *business-like* as any other major initiative of the organization. In a number of organizations, failed change processes have been treated as if they were *like-business*. That is, a senior executive might open up an off-site meeting with a few words of encouragement and then return to his or her office for his or her real work.

Travelling

Key groups must be seen to leave behind any complacency about maintaining the status quo and must reach out together for crucial learning about the what and how of continuous organizational improvement. The facilitators of the process must also be seen as risk takers in creating new learning experiences for those actually in and leading the change process.

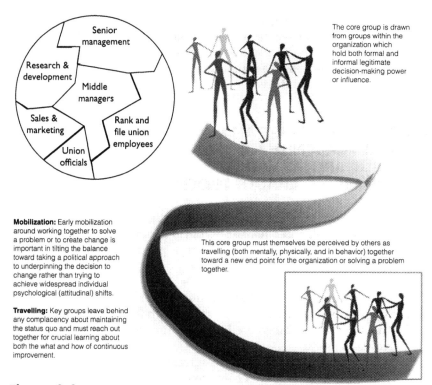

The core group is drawn from groups within the organization which hold both formal and informal legitimate decision-making power or influence.

Mobilization: Early mobilization around working together to solve a problem or to create change is important in tilting the balance toward taking a political approach to underpinning the decision to change rather than trying to achieve widespread individual psychological (attitudinal) shifts.

Travelling: Key groups leave behind any complacency about maintaining the status quo and must reach out together for crucial learning about both the what and how of continuous improvement.

This core group must themselves be perceived by others as travelling (both mentally, physically, and in behavior) together toward a new end point for the organization or solving a problem together.

Figure 3.3 Mobilizing a Critical Mass for Change and Travelling to a New Place

In Multi-Site Programs

In multi-site programs, this means bringing the best available learning experience to a common (neutral) place where all the key persons from all of the participating companies/sites can hear and discuss the experience together.

In Single Site/Company Initiatives

In single-site/company initiatives travelling can mean bringing the leaders of the change group from their home base to the location of the best and most relevant experience within or outside the region or country or even further afield as appropriate.

Travelling, as in conceptually accepting discomfort while identifying and absorbing valuable learning, is important for a balanced group from each setting. Determining what is crucial—*good to be pursued and bad to be avoided*—is the challenge to good facilitation. Additionally, the facilitator's challenge is to secure sufficient commitment to get the body of people to do things together and succeed. At the same time, he must provide training as needed as an important support mechanism once some changes have been introduced.

CONSCIOUSLY CREATE AND PROVIDE FOR A NUMBER OF PUBLIC ARENAS WITHIN EACH WORKING CHANGE PROCESS

Creating and maintaining public arenas for the use of all participating interest groups builds in a necessary transparency within the process of change. Here are a few arena maintenance principles that will help to maintain the integrity of the joint process:

1. All issues remain public (open to all parties).
2. Resource persons (experts) operate only on the public stage.
3. Analysis and decisions are built only on what emerges in public proceedings.
4. In the absence of a public arena, agreement, consultation, and negotiation arenas can easily become confused.

Items and topics which should be aired in the public arena include:

- The development and sharing of agreed objectives for change
- The production of flexible plans to underpin the change
- The monitoring and sharing of the successes and failures experienced
- Assessing and reporting on the changes introduced and the process initiatives undertaken
- Issues that remain public; they are shared only between the participating core groups
- Resource persons that operate only on the public stage; they are not available for private consultancies
- Analysis and decisions that are built only on what emerges in public proceedings, i.e., people can only share and give acknowledgement to change that has actually been introduced. Talking about what might have been achieved doesn't cut much ice.

Public Workshops

Crucial to the success of any Shared Learning process are workshops, which in the Integrated Rural Development case were held over the two-year period. These workshops are used to create the public arena, to share experiences, and to acquire training requested by the participants for the specific Shared Learning project.

Workshop Structure

Each workshop of the Integrated Rural Development program was attended by all core groups, core group coordinators, and the planning team. The agenda for each varied as the program proceeded but the general intention was to

- Exchange ideas
- Report on experiences
- Inspire and motivate those involved through contact with the examples and achievements of others (both from within and outside Ireland)

The timing and agendas for the workshops were designed to

- Set an ambitious pace for achieving results
- Communicate a work ethic and seriousness of purpose
- Provide a forum for demonstration of results achieved and difficulties or obstacles overcome

The Importance of the Workshops

Scheduled workshop activity for all the core groups is an important networking activity. The workshops play a huge role in shifting both individual and group thinking and behaviors toward the jointly desired change and future. The end result is that the workshops functionally set standards for groups to compare with their own experiences and accomplishments.

During the first Shared Learning project (organizations all introducing participative work processes within their organizations) the design called for all core groups attending four strategically timed workshops during the two-year period.

Each workshop went on for $2^1/_2$ days. Originally called workshops, they were colloquially known as *sweatshops* because people had to work for their change and were sharing their experiences (warts as well as beauty marks) with all of the other core groups. Three of them took place during the first half of the project. The third workshop fell on the birthday of the first workshop. The fourth event came at the end of the two-year period. The workshop timing was tied to this reasoning:

Going into something new or dangerous, you need support at the beginning—as much of it as you can get—and to know that you have a place to go where there are others who are suffering the same kind of loneliness.

Workshops in any type of Shared Learning application conform to the key principles associated with maintaining a public arena:

- Issues remain public, i.e., they are shared only between the participating core groups.
- Resource persons operate only on the public stage, i.e., they are not available for private consultancies.
- Analysis and decisions are built only on what emerges in public proceedings, i.e., people can only share and give acknowledgement to change which has actually been introduced.

CORE GROUPS ARE PAIRED/TWINNED WITH UNLIKE GROUPS TO ENHANCE OVERALL LEARNING

My first notion that Shared Learning was a distinct and advantageous manner of learning came, as I noted earlier, when we saw the leap in terms of depth and application of learning that came when outside groups or strangers asked questions of each other. Asking naive and/or *non-comfort zone* questions enabled people to focus on how key decision making processes and structures could either advance or retard change. It also meant that individuals and groups would be questioned about things they no longer asked about, but perhaps should have been. In other words, it drove people to look at themselves in a new light and assisted in the search for innovative answers or solutions.

In the first Shared Learning program, we established five sets of *twinned* organizations, in both the Republic of Ireland and in Northern Ireland, to facilitate networking across sectors, between public and private sectors, and also between various industries. Pairing unlike organizations together was important, because in this way they could support contacts and really focus together on the human dimension of the change process, which was the one thing they really had in common. If we had twinned one electric utility with another electric utility, they would quickly have found a level of comfort together, about the cost of crude oil, or coal, or the price per kilowatt; and this would have prevented them from making progress.

During the second Shared Learning program, *twinning* visits between pairs of rural area core groups were used to enhance process working and networking on a project-to-project basis. Meetings between those with specialized interests formed another sector in the public arena where technical and other details were exchanged openly between the participants.

ENOUGH TRUST, AS DISTINCT FROM ABSOLUTE TRUST, MUST BE MAINTAINED BETWEEN THE PARTICIPANTS

Trust, we have found, is certainly not something that can come out of any training program or simulation. Trust, it turns out, is always the by-product of honoring agreements about how you are going to work together and how decisions are made.

Consistent process is what counts! Trust may be enhanced in many different ways, but nothing beats consistently adhering to joint decisions and declarations made at the outset over the *who, what, where,* and *how* decisions affecting all of the parties working on change. All sorts of changes in the plan of work can be made and tolerated in the light of experience or a changed external environment as long as those changes adhere to the agreed upon *rules of the game* as they are embodied in enabling statements or charters.

In the numerous successful Shared Learning programs, many genuine surprises were produced from the most unlikely sources within these programs, so much so that if one had been overly judgmental about the specifics at the outset of any program and had been simultaneously a betting person, the picking of winners in advance would have been as hazardous as that faced by the tipster in any ten-horse race. This confirms that a consistent process is the most important aspect of change management.

HIGH-PROFILE PROCESS LEADERSHIP AND INTERACTION BETWEEN KEY INDIVIDUALS OF THE JOINT STEERING GROUP IS CRITICAL FOR SUCCESS

Looking back on a number of Shared Learning programs, high-profile process leadership and interaction between key individuals of the joint steering group provided purposeful motivation within a change process and toward their eventual success. In each case, local or on-the-ground ownership was fully achieved, and systematic and ongoing involvement by members of the joint steering group was necessary to keep the process going.

Joint leadership of the process outlasts (particularly from the continuity of process perspective) the contribution of an individual or charismatic leader within programs dedicated to permanent culture change. Promoting this nuance as a distinction within an overall concept of leadership without losing the decisive contribution and visionary potential of individual leaders, where they existed, was much more easily understood when the methodology was first generated within the multi-site/multi-community situation. Clearly, any individual was incapable of extending personal influence on outcomes within an initiative engaging ten separate organizations in two different Euro-economic regions (North and South of Ireland in pre-peace time).

It Provides for Alignment between Those with Clear and Legitimate Access to Power

On a site-by-site basis, a judgement of the potential of the networking contributors to become aligned with the vision of the future competitiveness of each situation was made at the highest level (CEO for the individual organizations involved). Following this largely intuitive decision (taken by the management figurehead and confirmed by those in leadership roles in other institutionalized groupings), the leading roles adopted by nominees from within the key interest groups in the best examples were forged into a common approach to jointness. In this way, a number of committed individuals with clear access to power (either positive or negative, proactive or reactive) agreed to agree with one another and to declare together the results of their joint activities. In these situations, overall process leadership to achieve change was enhanced and not diminished.

THE *HOW* OF DIFFUSING RESULTS, DECISIONS AND IMPLEMENTATION SHOULD BE AN INTEGRAL PART OF THE PROCESS OF CHANGE

We must always *walk the talk*, according to the hypothesis that: *The introduction of successful change depends on the way each proposal is structured:*

- Who participates in the problem solving and planning process
- What rules are applied
- What relationships are implemented

The Shared Learning design, as it has evolved over the years, provides repeated opportunities for *walking the talk* and continuously creating and recreating enough trust to successfully continue the process. Accordingly, from the outset, the active Shared Learning participants will be the ones (not experts and/or public affairs *translators*) who will actively participate *(walk the joint talk)* in introducing the changes and report to their peers on the ongoing process, as well as in the solutions to be implemented throughout the organization.

Recall that in each Shared Learning program there are a number of workshops, as well as ongoing individual work by core groups and sharing between those twinned groups between the scheduled whole group public arenas. During the workshops, core group meetings, and meetings between twins, it is the active participants, not experts or facilitators, who are

- Deciding directions for change and the initial processes underpinning such change
- Presenting and re-presenting these to each other in the public arenas of the program
- Formulating explanatory content about historical relationship difficulties
- Presenting joint intentions/plans/decisions
- Sharing the evolving plans, recorded achievement, and failure with comparators as peers and within concurrent timeframes
- Letting the leaders lead, participate, and share

At the end of the Shared Learning process, the perception should be it was the participants rather than the facilitator or experts who led the sharing of their experience and promulgated the usefulness of the processes involved.

For diffusion and/or implementation the approach should be:

- Use the experts for their expertise alone, particularly at the design and early stages of the change process.
- Use the direct-participant change agents as the people to communicate and convince other audiences to embrace change in the future.

This approach acknowledges that blockages to diffusion and implementation from site to site are probably more likely to occur because of workplace politics rather than workplace attitudes.

The emphasis is to create opportunities within which actual learners can share experiences with one another rather than allow training specialists to design communications arenas within which process experts attempt to train others in the knowledge, skills, and attitudes of change management.

The Facilitator's Role

The role of the process facilitator/change expert is to act as the designer and redesigner of the process for those involved in and leading the process itself. In a number of cases, all design and redesign work is done with the steering group off-site and the redesign presented by the steering group participants to the core groups without the facilitator/expert being present.

Facilitators should not be concerned about the fact that considerable uncertainty and apprehension is widely in evidence at the outset of a Shared Learning change process. They can with confidence work toward a situation where the rigor of the overall design and the inevitability of the timeframe implications and reporting expectations within the evolving public arenas of the process will produce effective outcomes rather than procedural correctness often considered more important in historical change models.

Facilitators should constantly remind themselves that participative change management is at most an art form in which they have a temporary and indirect mandate and is not a science or an ideology. Participative change management should facilitate the promotion of mixed competence and diversity as strength and as such should be regarded as being pluralist in its intent.

The *golden rule* for organizational design specialists/facilitators during a Shared Learning process should be something like this: *If anyone in the room looks to you when a significant process or content question is raised or when the air grows thick with tension, your profile is too high and the profile of those who are jointly leading the change process is too low.*

AN ESTIMATE OF WHAT OUTCOMES OR REWARDS WILL ACCRUE TO THE DIFFERENT PARTICIPANTS/STAKEHOLDERS SHOULD BE MADE EXPLICIT

Rewards: What's in It for Us/Me?

In other words, some formulation of *What's in it for us/me* as a reward or outcome should be estimated and shared at the most appropriate stages in the evolving process. Where clarification of this matter is called for, it may be faced up to in an open way within the enabling statement or compact agreed between the parties. Rewards, as understood here, can be divided between process and content rewards.

Process Rewards   The cycles of feedback themselves (the various public arenas of the change program) should confirm that genuinely collaborative arrangements in the pursuit of substantively important goals, can deliver significant results. When independent evaluation and assessment—which I highly recommend—is built into the process, it can confirm this judgement. Direct acknowledgements of contributions within the building of proposals for change and increased complementary skills that build personal competence and demonstrate enhanced flexibility of individuals and groups and growing self sufficiency in joint problem solving will also contribute to intrinsic satisfaction by participants for their part in the process.

Content Rewards   When proposals directly identifiable with the process make up the content of the changes introduced, a number of rewarding outcomes accrue:

- *For the employer:* Enhanced and sustained competitiveness and ongoing provisions for continuous improvement, etc.
- *For the employee:* Specific commitment to develop and negotiate terms of progressive wage systems (pay for knowledge within future flexible working arrangements). Commitment to make serious provisions for employment security and policies for training and retraining of job holders in situations of unavoidable labor force adjustment, etc.

Engaging and rewarding participants at the early stages of the process where outcomes or payoffs are not yet achieved or measurable may be still accomplished by noting the various steps taken, or *travelling,* done to arrive at the enabling statement.

In our first North-South multi-industry process, potential confusion was avoided within one of the companies in the program when agreement was reached on the following statement:

"The company and unions recognize also the separate roles of the negotiating and participatory functions. Participation, while it involves a commitment to common good and to the development of effective solutions in a cooperative fashion, does not inhibit the collective bargaining process which takes place separately. Equally, the collective bargaining process does not inhibit the effective development of ideas processed by participatory groups. Participation reflects the shared interests of achieving company effectiveness while collective bargaining reflects the distinct interests when sharing the benefits of company effectiveness."

When this statement was accepted by both sides they could see that each side had already *travelled* a good distance toward working together on joint interests.

SOME CLOSING THOUGHTS

What Is Potential of Shared Learning?

The excitement by the late Prof. Keith Thurley of the London School of Economics, when commenting on the results of the inaugural multi-site

Shared Learning program (in which he played an important part) was stated in this way:

> "Shared Learning is exciting and inspirational and it is now clear that it is more effective than discrete or individual company projects."

Professor Thurley was at that time synthesizing the views of the twenty or so international expert contributors in this first program into a composite view about the potential of the approach. He stated in response to the question, "What is its potential?":

1. It taps existing resources which are otherwise wasted.
2. Given #1, it is relatively inexpensive.
3. It is very relevant for situations calling for strategic change.
4. It can be used in groups of companies or within one large organization.
5. It can provide mass attack on problems.

What Has Shared Learning Demonstrated?

1. After slow take-off, fast change is possible.
2. Core groups can produce effective solutions.
3. A fuller use of human talent/capacity depends on a critical mass of support.
4. Innovation requires proactive education (to provide new ways of seeing old problems).
5. A prior condition for change is to raise expectations and standards.
6. Innovation needs comparators.
7. Through its carefully structured networking design, it allows participants to create and recreate enough trust to fully engage themselves in cooperative/collaborative work toward jointly supported ends.
8. Shared Learning is robust enough to work well in different organizational cultures, as well as across different national cultures.

Shared Learning and the Need to Face Ongoing Change

One of the greatest strengths of Shared Learning lies, perhaps, within the power of one of its seemingly paradoxical aspects:

> The conscious setting of limits for a process, liberates its participants.

Shared Learning works well to a large extent because it creates boundaries for the change process. Executives, supervisors, and frontline workers alike are freed, within the agreed-upon *rules of the game* to put forth focused effort for a set period of time to move the organization in a direction that all agree is beneficial.

We Don't Have to Sign Up for Life to Any Change Process but We Know We Will Need to Change Again   A recent Shared Learning experience with an electronics manufacturer has brought forth a somewhat new wrinkle in its application. (I say somewhat new because it relates back, in some ways, to the first two European pilot projects. More about this in a moment.)

The electronics firm knew from the start that *Shared Learning* set boundaries and had a definite beginning and ending. They developed and signed off on an enabling statement for a labor-management partnership to accomplish set goals. Then, after the core groups were already working on the change and looking forward to the first workshop six months hence, ongoing feedback between the participants and their stakeholders told them they had missed making these relationships clear.

They then reconvened to revisit the enabling statement, which they viewed as being a permanent draft. An addition to accompany the enabling statement was constructed to include the following language:

> "One of the key strengths of a progressive company in the modern world is its *ability to be flexible* in responding to its business environment and to have a positive outlook on the need for and the nature of change—a partnership approach will be crucial in order to underpin such flexibility. . . . *Partnership in this context* where pressure of time is crucial, *will be developed so that process delays or disagreement will not prevent progress and sometimes direct management action will be appropriate to maintain the momentum for change.* Any difficulties will be addressed in later review sessions and the spirit of cooperation preserved. Leadership will be required to overcome obstacles and the uninhibited access to collective bargaining arrangements will always be available if/where necessary."(emphasis added)

This added language demonstrates that they realize that even though they are signing up for one set of change only, new and unforeseen needs for change are likely to appear. And when that time comes they will use a "new" Shared Learning process to address it. In other words, they have selected targeted or boundaried partnership and Shared Learning as their permanent way of dealing with change. To accommodate this need, this Shared Learning process will now include increasing the firm's capacity for change by training employees of the firm to act as Shared Learning facilitators in the future. This firm's decision may be saying to us that in the future, we may see a number of organizations who will decide to adopt the Shared Learning process as their focused or *boundaried* vehicle for change.

How does this firm's choice to use Shared Learning repeatedly relate to the first two Shared Learning projects? The first Shared Learning project was used to successfully introduce employee involvement processes into a number of different firms simultaneously. It is not much of a stretch to imagine government, business, and labor jointly deciding (as some communities in the United States have with community quality councils) that the Shared Learning process should be used repeatedly to introduce quality and participation processes into all of the significant organizations in a community to enhance their ability to maintain and attract business.

Similarly, the Integrated Rural Development (IRD) project could be repeated in additional rural districts as an economic development planning vehicle and catalyst. We envision it being used a second and third or fourth time in the same communities to build upon, or extend the successes of its first application. In fact, the IRD project was seen somewhat in that manner: We trained a number of facilitators in the Shared Learning methods and principles to demonstrate that additional rural economic development projects could be launched simultaneously as funding became available.

Ten years may seem like a long time to test out a process. Yet these ten years have shown us just the potential of the Shared Learning process. We know in what types of settings and circumstances it works well and what the most important design principles appear to be. What we have to look forward to, and what I invite the reader to join with me in, is to discover new areas for its use and to demonstrate to a still skeptical world that competent, mature, ordinary people can through participative process make effective and valued change for their communities and their organizations.

Tom Lyons is a senior adviser with the Irish Productivity Centre in Dublin, Ireland, where he specializes in organizational and community development work. He is the originator of the Shared Learning process which is currently acknowledged as a leading change process initiative for Europe.

Author's Note: Over the years, somewhere between 150–500 people have taken different parts in the overall leadership roles in these programs for change. Numbers of them were specialists from centers of excellence with national and international reputations who provided important input and feedback. Additionally, many others with direct experience of change in well-known and regarded case histories in other cultures shared with us many important practical and tactical insights. The largest number of this overall cadre were ordinary job holders or community activists who were working in or living in the participating organizations and subregions in both the multi-site projects and single company initiatives. Where the designs were open ended, it is to this overall body of semi-anonymous people that we continue to be grateful for their participation over the years. As formal pilot projects, in the inaugural examples, our grateful thanks are due to the civil servants in the Irish Government Departments of Enterprise & Employment and Agriculture and those in Directorates General V and VI of the European Commission in Brussels who approved and sustained these initiatives through the provision of critical funding and support in successive budgetary periods.

EDITOR'S NOTE:

There is a story about quality and communication that begs to be told here:

> An American purchasing manager, who has just finished taking a quality course, adds a note on an order for 1 million diodes: "Please supply at 6 defects per million." When the shipment arrives it is accompanied by a small packet with the shipping documents and note attached. "In the small packet, you will find the 6 defective diodes you ordered from us. In the large shipping crate, you will find 999,994 diodes without defects. Please tell us, if you will, what you plan to do with the 6 defective diodes — our manufacturing manager said it was very difficult to make them defective."

There is of course, more than one joke here, but it illustrates quite well how crucial good communications are to any business process.

When researchers report that two-thirds to three-quarters of popular change programs fail to meet the goals or expectations of the organization, I am tempted to conclude that many more of these failures can be attributed to poor or no communications planning rather than to a lack of commitment by senior management and staff. I say that with confidence because of the hundreds of organizational and, consultant-produced TQM plans I have reviewed, I can't remember one that included any serious attempt at communications planning, or any detailed in communications process to support and maintain the change process.

Kaat Exterbille provides for us in Chapter 4 perhaps the most precious part of the change process puzzle: a process and examples of how to integrate communications planning into your change process. We should count ourselves fortunate that Exterbille is as well versed in change management as she is communications planning and practice.

Some readers will recognize the concepts as being very close to those used to communicate with customers about your products and services. Very good. Kaat's first message should be that we should take internal process management as serious as we do our advertising and marketing research, but she is perhaps more diplomatic than I.

After reading her contribution, you should be able to see how you can use existing communications expertise within your organization to help you take your change and improvement processes to much higher levels of success. Indeed, you will also be able to see how communications are an integral part of making things run well.

Chapter 4

"Follow Me! Say . . . Where Is Everyone?"

Kaat Exterbille, Kate Thomas & Kleyn

Just in case you missed it, the news is out: Today's employees and leaders seem to have split personalities:

- Many employees are not quite as willing as they were in the past to follow you off into the dark unknown or to go along with all your new ventures without questions—and a lot of them, at that.
- Many leaders see that they need to radically change how they adapt and act in their marketplace.
- Other leaders, companies, and employees have insulated themselves from the world and think nothing has changed, nor needs to change.

TODAY'S PROBLEMS

Employees Who Feel Trapped in the Dark Side of Work

Many employees feel that the unspoken (and sometimes written) social or corporate contract is, at the least, a bit threadbare and at the most, perhaps ripped beyond repair. The old corporate contract, which guaranteed job security and career possibilities in return for commitment and hard work, seems now to be a thing of the past. The result of seemingly unending waves of downsizing, mergers, and globalized competition reports, often accompanied by torrents of reports of radical cost cutting, offering early retirements to or laying off veteran employees, and demands for concessions from unions is a high degree of employee cynicism.

Leaders Who Feel and
See the White Heat of Competition

At the same time, many leaders realize that, now more than ever, they desperately need hard-working, flexible, and imaginative people with considerable experience and knowledge who are willing to fully commit themselves to working in new ways so as to assure both their success and the success of their company. Indeed, the word has gone out from some quarters that everyone should be an entrepreneur within the context of his or her own work process.

Leaders and Employees Wrapped in Grey Cocoons

As real and measurable external turbulence increases, within many of our more established companies, leaders and employees consider their place of work more and more as a snug little cocoon. Indeed, when you walk along the corridors of cocooned companies, the impression you get is that you are walking from one living room to another. The offices are really cozy-looking places with nice potted plants, photos of the kids, posters on the wall showing dream-like idyllic resorts and a box stuck in front of the door barring access to any unwanted visitors! The people who work in these offices-cum-living rooms may, from time to time, need to have a little chat with their colleagues, but they just don't seem to ever get around to it. It's just too nice, safe, and cozy in their little room to go outside. The cocooned leader or employee takes pride of place, and as often as not, the company seems to comes second.

Motivation and Commitment
in Split Personality Organizations

In the good old days, yelling "Crisis!" or "It's crunch time!" would get everyone's attention and get the company moving—but no more. In the good old days you could count on the energy of computer whiz kids or sales people to energize everyone—but no more. Saying that in your organization, people are the most valuable asset used to encourage commitment from those who were habitually continuous learners—but no more.

However, even though the times are turbulent and have caused much anxiety and cynicism, the questions employees have are the same as before:

- How well is the company faring compared with the competition?
- Am I on the winning side?
- Can I learn a lot here?
- Can I enhance my market value here?
- What do they expect from me?

- What are the standards?
- How am I doing generally?
- What is my position in this company?

For the leader, the proposition is the same as it always has been: If you can answer these questions effectively, your organization has a chance of succeeding. The problem is that in the good old days, the reality of half–hearted or slipshod communication was obscured by the generally rising tide. This time, and for the foreseeable future, the very survival of your organization depends on your ability to plan and deliver an effective communication process.

EFFECTIVE COMMUNICATION— AN ESSENTIAL MANAGEMENT TOOL FOR ADAPTING TO TURBULENT TIMES

Whatever type of change one considers (merger, takeover, rightsizing, process re–engineering, total quality management, or empowerment), from a communications standpoint these are all situations where the following four elements come into play:

- Shared values
- Mutual interests
- Continuous learning
- Personal positioning

Where to Start?

The pressure points in different change scenarios are often the same but depend on timing and style of leadership, the situation in each case may be different.

A Merger Example   In the context of a merger, as soon as the transition period is over, the vision of the new company must be communicated clearly and a clear declaration must be made by one person who has full authority and accountability to back up the statements. In short, the vision of the company must be backed up by firm leadership so staff can rally round and move forward unitedly.

Launching a Quality Program   When a quality program is launched, people tend to be cautious. They don't know what is expected of them and more often than not, they are not given an overall framework or a clear picture of the envisaged change. The management, meanwhile, does not provide a role model. Communications concerning the change are often reduced to a few brief words—a slogan. The result is a staff that has the impression that it's just another program or project. Consequently, conflict erupts in some places and nothing happens in other parts of the company because nobody knows exactly where they stand or in what direction they should be looking. To say the least, in such a situation, it becomes very difficult to maintain commitment in the company.

This offhand approach to communication is one of the reasons for the dwindling success of Total Quality Management (TQM). While the performance of TQM was still relatively high in 1986 (it achieved a satisfaction rate of 75% and was the third most commonly used change management technique), the level of management satisfaction has since dropped significantly.

In 1996, the techniques preferred by companies are mission statements and customer surveys. Even in this area, however, most successes will be short-lived unless there is proper communication and unless we have the courage to face up to the fact that the interests of the staff and the way they cooperate within a corporate culture are essential change parameters that must be properly taken into account within a constantly evolving market.

ADAPTIVE MANAGEMENT REQUIRES A MIXTURE OF COMMUNICATION AND CULTURAL CHANGE

A change in the psychology prevalent within the company can only be effected by making real changes in the organization that impact the way work is done and what work is done. Tangible and visible elements must go hand-in-hand with continuous communication on the expected attitudes and behaviors. In other words, the question, "What will the organization look and feel like?" must be answered.

Communication Must Be Considered in Its Broader Context

We are all familiar with the usual forms of communication—brochures, company videos, and newsletters. The most important communication method available in an organizational change is the organizational pay/reward system.

Another direct way of making the staff understand clearly what attitudes and behaviors they should demonstrate is to assess them on these factors in their annual appraisal. This may not be the most employee-friendly method, but it works. At any rate, the following year the staff will make sure they score higher on the appraisal of attitude and behavior changes.

When I say that this is perhaps not the most employee-friendly method, I mean that people have to change. But I assume that all employees are informed in advance, that they have the opportunity to assimilate this during a learning process, and that they have been shown examples. As soon as you measure anything and introduce standards, people tend to assimilate things more easily because the process has become more concrete and tangible.

Another important communication tool is style of leadership, in other words, the power of exemplary behavior. Ongoing management behavior is the most powerful communication instrument in any organization. On average, the staff give the impact of management behavior a rating of 75% compared with the mere 4% given to the impact of conventional communication supports such as company publications.

Communication Is Not Simply a Matter of Conveying a Message

In this new era before us, where customer focus, empowerment, teamwork, and so on are vital elements for success, it is not enough simply to feed information through the system, a process which is effected mostly through company publications.

The business world in turbulent times calls for a new approach to communication. Informal communications will and have to increase. People are becoming more critical, better able to stand up for themselves, and better trained. In addition, as they have access to their own electronic communication channels, they will be able to send their own messages faster and more frequently than in the past.

The long and short of communications in turbulent times is this: Management can no longer control and or direct the communication environment. Consequently, more than ever they will have to convey to the staff the company's image of the future instead of trying to control communication. In addition to task-oriented communication, policy-oriented communication will take on particular importance among process owners. Furthermore, the focus of communication will shift away from marketing communication towards corporate communication. Ethical values, for example, the company's management of the environment, will become increasingly important not only for the staff of the company but also for the outside world.

The forms of information are changing. We are seeing continuous development in the various forms of communication. There is less and less interest in literature and written communication. Due to information overload, people are increasingly guided by pictures and instantaneous impressions as well as short, arresting messages and ideas. In short, people are not willing to devote their time and energies to long-winded stories. There will be more and more interest in, and need for, direct communication, that is, interpersonal and face-to-face communication.

The Image of the Sender, Whether or Not a Blood Brother or Sister, Is Becoming Increasingly Important

In effect, who says it is often more important than what is actually said. The result, everyone will have to enhance:

- Their interpersonal communication skills
- Their ability to convey messages in layman's terms
- Their ability to motivate co-workers

At present, this is not the strong point of any of our management teams. A survey among participants at an executive program in the Wharton School revealed that communication was the second skill management lacked after the formulation of their strategy.

Communicating with vision is becoming more and more important. I purposely refer to management with vision rather than management with leadership because leadership is often confused with a style one associates with a smooth-talker and extrovert who makes ambitious and visionary declarations and surrounds him or herself with a cohort of equally smooth-talking Young Turks. The good news is that you can give new direction to your organization by bringing about a change in the mentality or collective vision of the staff within your organization. The not-so-good news is that no outside consultants can do this for you and that there are barriers to overcome.

BARRIERS TO INTERNAL COMMUNICATION WITHIN ORGANIZATIONS

The barriers to internal communication can be subdivided into three pressure points:

- Strategic
- Operational
- Cultural

Strategic and Operational Pressure Points

Internal communications about change are seldom linked to the strategic company plan. Often these messages do not even go hand-in-hand with actual, tangible changes. As a result, employees receive many of these internal communications as mere lip service because few, or no, clear statements contain objectives or measurable results. Within the context of a merger, the question, "How will we be different and by what date?" is seldom addressed.

Cultural Pressure Points

The possession of information, or the right to freely communicate throughout the organization, is thought of as an instrument of power and/or control in most companies. However, this power is easily bypassed when the messages in the formal communications channels are slow, vague, or used infrequently or ineffectively. Everyone from top to bottom within the company openly criticizes internal communication when it is not working smoothly, but few take the time or trouble to use it well, or to use such channels to empower staff by giving them access to all the information they need to do their tasks well and to plan for the future.

Often people are unwilling to accept training or guidance in the field of communication because it is taken for granted that if you can write and speak, you can communicate. At other times, a lack of mutual trust among departments or levels results in the lower echelons keeping information back for fear they will have to work harder for no more reward or security. A lack of mutual trust can cause top and middle managers to not inform first-line workers of impending changes for fear that they will use the information against the company.

The most frequently made mistakes regarding communication of needed or impending changes are:

- Failure to start thinking about communication in good time
- Failure to phase or sequence the messages
- Failure to draw up a strategy

The result: The grapevine starts buzzing before any formal communication is made. And once the grapevine gets started, people begin pressing panic buttons and lunging at information without any prior research and without taking into account the wishes and ideas of the staff.

Proper Preparation Is
More Than Half the Battle

For the concept that internal communication is a genuine management instrument to be accepted, a planned approach is required. To this end, an internal communication strategy must be developed, particularly where the process will entail making changes to corporate culture.

In my work I use a planning cycle to work out this strategy on the basis of collected and existing data. The core of the model is a recurring audit process of information collection and analysis. Based on these analyses, long-term and intermediate problems are clearly defined and pressure points are identified.

The standard pressure points are usually of a strategic, structural, or cultural nature. However, other pressure points may be formed by

- The external environment
- The product and services supplied
- Communication in the broadest meaning of the term

In short, the style of management may also create pressure points. Without going any deeper into the actual research methodology, I must at this point also mention the different expectations of the quantitative and qualitative research methods:

- Quantitative, questionnaire-based research is less appropriate at the outset but nonetheless offers the advantage that it provides a means of quantifying the answers and offers a reference point or zero measurement point for later use. With this method we can determine whether all the efforts that have been undertaken have resulted in a change in the outlook or behavior of the target group.
- The preferred types of qualitative research used in the first phase of the planning cycle are in-depth interviews and focus groups:
  —In-depth interviews can be used to garner more factual information.
  —Group discussions can, by their brainstorming character, yield very creative ideas. At the same time, this process provides a form of therapy for the participants through social interaction. Consequently, it is best to carry out quantitative research after qualitative research.

The Employee-Focused Approach to Communication Planning

We take as a given that employees cannot be considered as a homogenous whole and that there is a need to assess the needs, learning styles, and starting points for different groups of employees. However, there is no universally applicable way of subdividing staff because every organization is different.

The world of advertising may offer some clarification in this respect. Before a new convertible is launched on the market, for example, it is essential to determine whether it will appeal to female or male buyers. If the target group is defined as female, it is advisable to ascertain the specific needs of this group, further subdividing it perhaps into women with children and those without children. We have exactly the same problem with each company. We must ask the staff:

- What they expect from the company
- How they see things generally

- How they see the market
- How they would assess the policy implemented up to that point
- To what extent they would be willing to agree to changes.

  Additional questions for staff might include:

- What is the corporate culture?
- What is the style of leadership?
- How do they view the organizational structure, procedures, systems, and resources?
- What is the information culture?
- What is the communication structure (internal and external) in three areas: written communication, behavior, and use of symbols?
- What do they expect from the company and what is important for the individual members of staff?
- Is there a credibility gap between the values and standards of the company and those of the staff?

The Customer-Oriented Approach

This type of research can also be carried out among customers. Being customer-oriented means fulfilling the expectations of your customers. First and foremost, we must understand what customers want and determine whether we are fulfilling these expectations. (These are the basic objectives of the conventional market research methods.)

Within the framework of a TQM communications plan, for example, we go one step further than conventional market research by determining what the customer values most (friendliness, ease of access to service or product, etc.) and defining service standards on this basis. All too often changes are implemented in an organization solely on the basis of what the organization thinks the needs of the customer are. The danger, of course is that all our efforts will totally escape the notice of the customer.

Some firms, even though they are careful in their marketing research and familiar with the planning cycle, do not think to apply these same processes when introducing change within their firm. Positive results can be achieved if we make strategic partners of our staff, as well as our customers. This research method starts a process that ultimately leads to a learning organization because the standards that are set in relation to staff can in turn be applied to the customers, or vice versa.

Just-in-Time and Customized Message Delivery

People must be ready for change. Therefore, a schedule is essential. But the plain fact that nobody is interested in a subject if it doesn't really concern them means that any information directed toward them must also be delivered on time; it must also be specifically geared towards the specific target group.

WHAT YOU WERE MAY TELL YOU
WHAT TO EXPECT OF TOMORROW

So far, we have looked at the external environment and the internal environment of your organization, but this does not really offer a sufficient basis upon which to develop your communications strategy for change. Some of the most important questions which are too often overlooked are:

- What is the history of the organization culture, or the history of, the company?
- Is the corporate culture geared towards the organization or geared towards people?
- Does the company give more consideration to people and values or does it assign greater importance to rules or individual performance levels?
- How is the company positioned in the market vis-a-vis its competitors?
- What success milestones can it look back to in the past?
- What is the company's track record in terms of changes?
- How many changes have the staff had to cope with recently, how were these changes introduced, and how successful were they in achieving their objectives?

Your communications program to support your planned change cannot be copied from a competitor, even if the other company operates in the same sector and the research carried out into employee satisfaction yields the same results. Your plan must be based on your history and experience. This taking inventory phase must lead to a strategic communications plan, later followed by an action plan.

The Change Communications Strategy

Before we craft a communications strategy, we must first decide what we want, what position we will adopt, and what kind of response we want from our staff or customers. The possible responses are:

- A desired rational response
- A desired emotional response
- Some form of behavioral response

At this point, the current position of the organization is mapped out and the policy to be implemented is defined in terms of objectives. The strategic choices as regards what will ultimately become the communication actions are made on the basis of the discrepancy between where we are and where we want to be, also referred to as *gap analysis*.

The main elements of the strategy consist of:

- Definition of the desired ultimate aim
- Definition of the core messages, which are usually divided into what I call *reactive messages* (doing away with prejudices) and *proactive messages* (emphasizing new elements and values)
- The relationship between the communication as a management instrument and other management instruments, which generally means those in the human resources sector such as salary, education, training, and co-determination or negotiated contracts (if applicable)
- The choice of the mode of communication or of the persons responsible for communication
- The setting of priorities or the phasing of the approach to the target groups taking account of the actual changes that are taking place.

Based on all these parameters, a communication resource program is defined in terms of tools such as newsletters, speeches, memos, and so on, which all compliment each other.

The Continuous Communications Improvement Process

The development of organizational learning is based on the introduction and monitoring of the process that provides a means of combining the visible and the measurable aspects of actual improvements with results in less tangible matters. To illustrate this point, when I am working with a client, we

1. Identify all the aspects that describe the market as a service.
2. Draw a comparison between the perception of the customers and the assessment of the staff of their own behavior.
3. Give a diagnostic description of this service as compared with other suppliers to all members of staff at their own level.

The advantage of this process is that the staff can compare themselves with their colleagues or with other companies in the marketplace.

Depending on the direction the company wishes to take, specific criteria will be defined along with a number of standards. Some concepts such as cost leadership are easy to measure, while others such as friendliness are somewhat more difficult to measure. However, it must be made digestible and practical for the staff, otherwise nothing changes.

This approach immediately yields usable results. It provides a means of comparing one's own performance with that of the competition. In addition, this comparison is made on the basis of the characteristics perceived by the customer as being important. We can also draw a comparison between the staff's perception of their own performance and that of the customers'. Corrections can be made by management or, better still, by the process owners. Depending on their long-term objectives, they can identify areas where their performance is lacking, what the cost would be if they were to implement this change, and whether it is worthwhile.

To summarize this section, I would like to mention a few tips that may be useful when it comes to setting up a new work environment:

- Focus the organization on the market and the customers.
- Consult your people before making any changes.
- Define your vision and be future-oriented.
- Set a course of action that can be understood and translate this in terms of the job of each individual.
- Segment your communication in terms of form, content and volume.
- Use the concept of process ownership. This will save time and lessen the fear of changes.
- Define success parameters and measurable results.
- Make tangible changes together with results in less tangible matters.
- Divert attention away from internal pressure points and don't indulge in navel-gazing.
- Set in place the practice of permanent listening. After all, communication is 50% listening and 50% talking.

To bring all that we have discussed into a clearer picture, I will apply it to the introduction of a TQM process.

TQM CAN BE DOA WITHOUT A PROPER COMMUNICATIONS PLAN

The introduction and maintenance of any quality and participation process is synonymous with change—changes in structure, working methods, corporate culture, and so on, down the line to the employee at the shipping dock or those who meet your customers on a daily basis.

Step 1: Communications Plans and Change

Above all, the communications plan has to address the question of what the organization as a whole wishes to achieve. Employees need to know why they are being exposed to, and expected to be a part of this change process. In short, the communications plan has to take into account:

- The potential contribution of every employee to the change process
- The hoped–for attitudes and behaviors of all those concerned
- The corporate culture one wishes to attain

"Here, Now You Do Something with This!" Doesn't Work

Oftentimes companies complete their TQM plans in the same manner as they used to complete their engineering plans: "When we're done with them, we just toss them over the wall to manufacturing" (read "communications" in this instance). So they say to their communications people, "Go communicate the TQM message." The result is brochures, posters, and training programs that may or may not make sense to the intended targets—the employees.

But what really matters is the impression the recipient gets of the TQM approach as a result of the communications effort—what is said, in what way, and via which channel or media, is of crucial importance. Your real starting point should be based upon this foundation:

> The viewpoint of the receiver of the message should be the starting point for your TQM communications process.

If Your Objective Is Really to Involve Employees   What is the difference between real communications and the simple transmission of information? Communicating with employees in a manner that encourages and invites them to think and act differently, rather than just saying what we think they should think, say, and do—that's the difference.

Your communications must start with your employees and should be adapted to their needs. The criteria for the effectiveness of your communications strategy should be:

- Are employees familiar with the quality and participation philosophy?
- Are employees ready to accept change?
- Are employees involved?

Target/Task-Oriented Preparation   The key change issues and the target individuals and groups (those who will carry out the changes) need to be clearly identified. Your first step is to consider what your employees' needs are before they will be prepared to commit themselves. To take that step, you need to answer these questions:

1. Who are our employees?
2. What do we expect from them?
3. What are their expectations of the organization?
4. What are their current attitudes?
5. What is the corporate culture?

The issues of quality and participation need to be evident in every communication if the change is to be taken seriously. After the preparation steps have been taken, we must look at integrating this change within the global corporate strategy. Since an organization's leaders are its chief integrators they are involved in the next step.

Step 2: Leadership's Role in the TQM Communications Strategy

The task of top management is to consistently make the link between the quality and participation strategy and the operational results required by the organization's global strategy. In short, talking about how operational results flow from the quality and participation strategy is top management's chief role in supporting quality and participation as a strategic means to overall success. Such messages should not, repeat, should not be limited to conventional corporate media (videos, newsletters, and memos), but should also be evident in day–to–day communications.

Next to a clearly stated strategy and implementation plan on what to communicate, the most important success factor in the communications plan is the conviction and powers of persuasion of every member of management.

TQM Communication—A Tool to Enhance Leadership   "TQM strikes at the very core of our business activity" is an often-heard statement. Our employees know this and they are sometimes even heard to echo these words themselves. However, this is not something they always experience because it does not affect all aspects of company activity. Instead:

- TQM ideas remain limited to TQM publications.
- TQM communication is restricted to the TQM meeting.
- TQM decisions remain confined to the project group and the contingent of direct superiors.
- And all too often, the TQM message is not put across with conviction by top management.

When the TQM appears in the title of a speech, the speaker will, of course, not fail to talk about TQM, but when some other topic is invoked, for example, human resources policy, the link with the TQM philosophy is not always explicitly made, whereas company employees expect, *if management is really serious*, that the link between TQM and the entire business activity be established on a regular basis.

If top management can effectively establish the link between TQM and company business across the board, we can be sure that it will not merely be a set of good intentions or a leap in the dark.

Before implementing TQM, be sure to

- Determine how TQM relates to the mission of the company.
- Train top management in the day-to-day translation of their vision of TQM into general company policy.
- Identify topics on which the TQM message can be conveyed.

These topics must be phased in otherwise there is a danger that everyone will start talking at the same time from different avenues of approach. For example, if we decide that a certain value should be incorporated in the company, this might serve as a leitmotif or as the topic of the month. We must identify communication topics that are derived from the process results. In other words, TQM is not only a matter of process optimization but also involves a change of mentality.

Step 3: An Effective TQM Communication Does Not Start with a Multi-Step TQM Implementation Plan

Before developing quality and participation skills and techniques, it has to be made clear why the quality improvement effort is in and of itself necessary and why active commitment and involvement in it is needed from every employee. The firm must answer at least these two questions:

- What company results indicate that a TQM process is needed?
- How does our competitive situation tell us that TQM is needed?

Only when these questions are answered in a manner that is understood by all should the approach to the quality issue be set out. Once the importance of the project is clear, then and only then will training in the different quality techniques be effective.

Training vs. Communicating   There is a lot of confusion surrounding the role/content of communication and that of training. Although the two must be set up in parallel, they are not interchangeable. Many companies start with an awareness phase. During this phase, the different techniques, procedures, and competencies commonly applied in the context of the TQM philosophy are described to the staff. In this context, awareness training means telling the staff how TQM processes must be initiated and what its steps actually entail. The answer to the crucial question, "Why should I get involved in TQM?" is never answered. The employees are given no background information on the market situation. The change in ethos essential for any change is often not disregarded. The right way to introduce TQM is to:

1. Tell your people why the company is implementing TQM—explain the role of the personnel.
2. Explain the participation of the personnel—explain the market situation.

At this point, and only at this point, you should explain "How we will go about TQM." The long and the short of what I am saying here is that the TQM awareness session and the TQM communication plan separate actions which must be set up in parallel.

Step 4: What Do We Want to Change and How Will We Subsequently Measure These Changes?

TQM communication is not an ad hoc task. It is a management tool to be used within the process of change. Communication and attitudes are difficult to measure and for that reason are seldom actually measured. A declaration of communication intent and the measurement process can in this regard form the basis for what will later become your benchmark instrument. Here are the basic questions to be answered by employees:

- What they expect from the company
- How they see things generally
- How they see the market
- How they would assess the policy implemented up to that point
- To what extent they would be willing to agree to changes

Measuring the Communication Process   As with any other strategic initiative, being able to measure whether goals are being achieved is important. Measurement techniques need to be envisaged to track the success of the communications process with benchmarks and key success indicators.

"What's in it for me?" The only effective way to get employees to buy into the quality philosophy is to make them fully aware of the personal advantages of this method, in other words, to communicate how their tasks will be more satisfying as they understand how their contribution leads to improved customer satisfaction and a more secure future.

On an ongoing basis, it is important to communicate continuously the results of the quality effort, as well as to give appropriate recognition to the individuals or teams who have achieved these results. Such recognition can take the form of small, not necessarily financial, awards as well as articles in the company magazine or even (what should have been normal) a simple thank you!

How Is Internal Communication Implemented during the TQM Phases?   There is no hard and fast rule in this case because this will to a great extent depend on the corporate culture and history of the company:

- Is the company experiencing change fatigue? Has your company recently undergone changes or restructuring, and, if so, how well were these changes received?

- Is the corporate culture geared towards the organization or towards people?
- In a company with a corporate culture geared towards people and values, the project-oriented TQM approach will form the basis of your communication.

In an organization that assigns considerable importance to roles and structure, an ISO manual is a very useful instrument. However, in a company where individual initiative and competition are more valued, the communication should be directed at individual performance, unless this will weaken or distort certain elements of corporate culture.

The Awareness Phase   This first phase involves explaining clearly why change is necessary. A mission statement setting out the values and goals of the company is an essential communications tool in this situation. Ideally the message will come directly from top management to everyone involved. At the same time, all managers need to receive background information and briefings in such a way that everyone tells the same story and that any bottom line explanations can be backed with facts and figures. The TQM mission is essential within the communication strategy

Kickstarting the Process   An important instrument that can be used to kickstart the TQM process is the dissemination of the TQM mission. The mission can be used to convey the desired values. It is also an instrument that allows the staff to make sure that they are looking in the same direction. In addition, it can be used as an arbitration instrument for those who are unwilling to follow and releases the pressure that may lead to situations that call for a charismatic leader.

An Acclimation Milepost   Employees need some period of time to identify with the new strategy. To ensure this, they need to be involved in the development of the strategy itself. Effective one-on-one communications are essential. The message should not just come from the top down. Since, employees the world over watch a leader's feet more closely than their lips, a key factor here is readiness by management to listen to the input from employees and to act accordingly. To facilitate this process, managers have to be coached in developing personal communications skills. Management has to set the right example in its attitudes and behavior.

Top Management Behavior   The staff members are under pressure and do not see exemplary behavior by top management. One of the classic mistakes that is made is that technical processes are optimized at the first opportunity but social processes are left lagging behind. Communication will usually involve controversial social issues and should therefore not be handled in an offhand or autocratic manner. In this regard, the optimization of communication supports and communication channels (for example, by making impeccable internal brochures or by optimizing internal communication channels) should not be regarded as a nonessential. When it comes to assessing communication channels, it is essential that the organization be viewed objectively, as it were, from a distance. In fact, this is a task that can best be carried out by an external agency as this form of process optimization may involve desecrating a number of sacred cows and stepping on people's toes.

The Adaptation or Implementation Phase Once employees have identified with and are ready to commit themselves to the mission, they need to hear clearly exactly how they can contribute. Two communications techniques are relevant at this stage: task–oriented and personally-oriented messages.

Using both task-oriented and personally-oriented examples, the mission has to be interpreted for every employee individually, while reflecting the corporate values and environment. Explanations of how strategic and operational applications of the mission benefit the day–to–day operations should be clear to both operational employees and human resources management and staff.

Staff members who are not involved in a project group often have a tendency to consider all the hoopla and to-do surrounding TQM is

Table 4.1 The Links Between The TQM Plan and the Communications Planning Function

Phase	Question	TQM action	Communications task
Preparation		• Top management meetings	• Establish a steering group • Employee research: Needs of target groups Perception of the organization
Awareness	Why change?	• Awareness sessions at all levels • Quality philosophy and methodology • Identification of process problem areas	• Desk research: Corporate vision/mission Corporate strategy • Provisional communications strategy and timetable
Process audit and adaptation	Why am I involved?	• Social Pareto • Social audit	• CEO message • Background briefings to line management

Table 4.1   Continued

Phase	Question	TQM action	Communications task
		• Technical Pareto	• Identification of social and management problems areas
Implementation	How do I do it?	• Project groups • Method of implementation	• Vision, TQM mission • One–on–one communications motivational platforms • Management communications skills Leadership training
	What do I have to do?	• Presentation to steering group	• Support for middle management • Optimize communications methods and media
Adoption	Are we doing it right?	• Cross–functional coordination • Adopt strategy • Strategic benchmarking • Re–engineering/work redesign	• Task-oriented communications Skills training Techniques Information on techniques Measurable tasks
		• Quality function deployment • Networking	• Person/individual-oriented communications Communication about the desired new culture and its values on quality and participation Feedback mechanisms and participation • Cross–functional communications • Benchmark research • Customer and employee research • Communications network • Human resources evaluation of values and contribution to culture.

something very remote from their day-to-day concerns. This is something that must be avoided. To this end, it is essential to set up initiatives or channels that not only provide the staff with information but also give the staff opportunities to participate in numerous different ways.

The Adoption or Internalization Phase Finally, there is the adoption or internalization phase. Staff is wondering how they have done, whether they have performed effectively:

- Has TQM become a system enabling constant improvements in productivity?
- Are all the strategic processes integrated within the TQM methodology?
- Have re–engineering projects which may have also been launched on the basis of a communication plan been integrated with the TQM communication plan?
- Have cross-functional consultation sessions been set up within the organization?

If these questions can all be answered positively, then this is the picture we should have before us:

- The customer has become a partner within the framework of the entire process and therefore has some say in any sessions, brochures, and so on.
- The need to satisfy the internal and external customer continues to be the constant driving force behind the process.
- The continuous benchmarking of communication processes, communication supports, corporate culture, and hoped-for attitudes and behavior patterns are now seen to be very much a part of the TQM philosophy.

A Final Word on Feedback Feedback on the new organizational culture should be continuous. Opportunities should also be provided so that employees can give their views on the overall quality program and get clarification of their individual roles. Even those employees not directly involved in project groups should be associated with the program by receiving information on both the results and the colleagues who have helped achieve them.

In reality, the steps described previously can never really be clearly defined in this way. Indeed, in most cases they will overlap. Within each company, there may be differences in the rate of change. Some people will adjust very quickly to changes while others will be more gingerly in their approach and may prefer to wait and see which way the wind blows. Given proper information flow, major gaps will be bridged. Early adapters will carry with them the more sluggish elements in your organization. The main thing is, of course, to identify the pullers in advance. In other words, it is important to know your organization before you implement the TQM policy.

CREATING A LEARNING, ACTIVELY ADAPTIVE ORGANIZATION

There is no recipe book when it comes to changing corporate culture. Like people, every organization has a distinct identity and personality, so much so that it is impossible to offer a universally applicable recipe for change. Nonetheless, we can gain some insight into the processes involved by considering a number of general guidelines. Changes in mentality do not take place overnight. Anyone who believes they can bring about change in corporate culture by setting up a half-baked TQM program at the drop of a hat one day, the following year, a re–engineering project and then the year after, a corporate rightsizing program, is more than likely in for a disappointment.

In fact, the management will have to work constantly to steer the ship in the right direction and to show the way ahead. This is a costly business, not just in terms of financial input but in terms of effort.

The Change Process at Evolution Textiles

The case outlined in this section is presented as an example of a successful corporate change. However, the exact approach we describe would perhaps not work in other firms unless it was in tune with the existing culture.

This case demonstrates how an integrated communications approach enabled the company to tap new markets, to downsize a department without any problems, and to set in place a culture for continuous improvement.

Evolution Textiles has just been through a rather rough patch. The company has several product lines: consumer textiles and upholstery for office and institutional (health care) furniture.

The firm was founded in 1950 and until 1985 was privately held. When acquired by an international holding company in 1985, it moved into the export market with its office and institutional product lines. The staff had for years felt they could look forward to a guaranteed job for life. All that began to change in 1985.

The Problem: Culture Clash

The problem which then developed was not that its new exports burdened the company; Evolution had already been exporting it base products for a number of years. The problem was that the different corporate culture of the holding company created insecurity within the company. In addition, the textiles sector was by now also under considerable pressure, profit margins were becoming increasingly tight, and the highly regulated health care industry was imposing more and more stringent standards. Industry was also becoming increasingly regulated at a national and regional level due to new environmental laws and labor regulations which followed one after the other during the early and mid-1980s.

Management Takes Stock of the Situation

Management at this point began to reconsider its raison d'être. It wanted to guarantee a secure future for the company and maintain a team spirit while respecting each person's individuality within the company.

First Attempts at Strategic Improvement Programs Flop

The company decided to try out improvement and strategic management programs but did not achieve the hoped-for results in terms of the set objectives, i.e., "security for the future and respect for each person's individuality." None of the consulting firms used had mentioned the need for research on the firm before setting off with new strategies.

When my firm was retained to assist them in recovering from their failed change programs, we first closely scrutinized the corporate strategy. In-depth interviews and focus groups where set up involving the staff and all the stakeholders. Since not all the staff could be interviewed, they were asked to identify, via a survey, the most common technical and social bottlenecks in their work environment. This ensured that everyone had some active involvement in the changes taking place in the organization.

The organization was not only looked at from the outside looking in but from the inside looking out, in terms of perception and in terms of the actual areas of difficulty. The people working within the organization and the external stakeholders were informed of the need for the research and the possible repercussions of this work on future work patterns and organization. We told them that we didn't know exactly where we were heading but that we wouldn't be doing anything behind anyone's back. An interim staff satisfaction survey conducted a few months later revealed that this approach and openness on the part of the management was very much appreciated. This quantitative survey also served as a zero reference point at a later date to assess staff satisfaction with the resulting program.

Gap Analysis and Vision Meetings

Internal and external market data were presented to the management or, to put it another way, management was confronted with the gaps between their perception of the market and the existing business plan and the data derived from the market. The future contours of the market and Evolution Textiles were discussed and defined with all first-line managers. Subsequently, a number of vision workshops were set up with the staff of the company.

During the course of these vision workshops and in consultation with senior management, new long-term strategies were formulated and operational actions implemented—some for the whole company, others just for one department or individual.

The decision was taken to realign Evolution's divisions/departments according to the needs of the market and customer:

- A department that was not part of the core business was eliminated.
- A department that at first glance appeared to be less profitable was retained and received more resources because the customers from other markets considered this department to be highly valuable and judged the creativity of the entire company on the merits of this department.

From the standpoint of corporate culture change, this approach was extremely valuable because the research work provided a basis for the setting of standards and a means of measuring the transformation taking place.

Collective Mindsetting and Operational Fine-Tuning

Now we get down to the nitty-gritty. It is simply not enough to set the new values in a nice, neat frame, cross your fingers, and hope that the staff will look at it and learn something from it. The concept of collective mindsetting implies that all the staff are forging ahead in the same direction as one. It means that everyone clearly understands the objectives and agrees to assume responsibility for achieving them in measurable terms.

The Role of Management at Evolution

These new corporate principles, which were the outcome of internal and external research and especially staff input, were communicated by top management during a kickoff event. This gave the staff the overall picture and demonstrated to the staff clearly that they stand four-square behind the new principles. Even though the input of the management decreased somewhat after that event, they received coaching on ongoing communication behavior which would bring home to staff what the desired behaviors were and how they would have to walk their talk. In addition, a communication action plan was drawn up for each manager, in accord with their own operational business plan, to make sure they are regularly reinforcing Evolution's principles for change.

Lower and middle management ultimately play a crucial role in translating these principles into a form that could be adopted by the different departments They are a vital linchpin and, if they so desire, they could simply scuttle the entire operation if their views are not properly taken into account. At Evolution Textiles, these levels were entrusted with the implementation of the corporate change program. It was made abundantly clear to them that they were the translators of the vision to each department. Indeed, it was they and they alone who could, as it were, translate for the staff how they might apply this new approach to their work environment. During the process at Evolution we developed many management letters, question-and-answer lists, and training sessions to assist lower and middle managers in their roles.

The Nuts and Bolts of the Communication Process

The kickoff event, which was attended by all, was supported by parallel communication. This mass communication process went hand-in-hand with the management communication that took place through the organization. Evolution developed a new corporate identity and logo to give the corporate image a facelift and as a peg on which to hang much of the communication going on in the company. After the kickoff event, where the mission statement manual was handed out, the staff left the room under a sea of flags bearing the new logo.

The next morning, the staff found on their desks a special issue of the company newsletter with an outline of the main changes along with a number of policies or tasks that were being done away with.

Employees who had no e-mail address promptly received one; e-mail messages served as a means of sending messages quickly to everyone but did not become the new communications tool for all uses. An e-mail user's manual was distributed to remind all staff that real communication (face-to-face and in dialogue) and e-mail information were very different from one another.

During the initial months, the communication was primarily top-down and involved a number of mass media instruments. But from the very outset, care was taken not to oversell the change program.

Communications in Critical Areas   Problem areas and people who were critical of the success of the program were monitored in advance and given an opportunity to air their views. Discussion platforms and work consultation processes were created to give people the opportunity to air their grievances in good time.

After some time, the communication tools were further segmented. Within each target group (department or work unit), workshops were set up to discuss communications, and the staff were able to put forward proposals concerning their own communication program. Throughout the entire process, the trade unions cooperated completely and undertook their own communications tasks.

Down with the Fortress Mentality! Death to Hierarchical Rituals!

Bureaucratic procedures and hierarchical rituals identified during the in-depth interviews (which were seen as impediments to change) were immediately replaced. Consultation and discussion platforms quickly became very much the order of the day.

Open house days were organized to give the staff an opportunity to learn about each other's jobs. Each department received a budget to present its activities in a visual manner by means of a display board, a stage presentation, or a simple get-together. A mini-country fair was set up in the entrance hall of the company with panels representing the different departments.

The Link to Human Resources

The new approach was also demonstrated through tangible and intangible incentives. The stated improvement criteria and accompanying standards were also included in the annual staff appraisal. Supervisors and managers received a memo outlining their cultural change and a evaluation plan to enable them to interpret the human change standards.

A number of staff ranking anomalies which had developed historically and been identified in the social Pareto were addressed one by one. As a result of top-down evaluations, the staff, management, and entire departments could see that there was a real need to improve interpersonal skills. The number of training courses in task-oriented and social skills was increased.

Processes at the Frontline

To set in motion a change in behavior, mentality, and culture, hierarchical superiors, foremen, and informal leaders were trained to conduct work consultation processes and to convey the messages effectively. The work consultation process sometimes took place on the shop floor and sometimes in the meeting room. In a few cases, this process was connected with external exercises which at first glance appeared to have nothing to do with the entire process. For example, the company set the corporate staff to build a raft to convey the message of team spirit.

Group leaders received advance training for their task: A large range of different tools was developed to help them to convey the subject matter effectively and flexibly. In particular, the staff themselves, with their concerns, queries, and interpretation of the new corporate values, played a central role in these communication instruments. After some time, we set up a number of heterogeneous groups (people from other departments, different levels, internal customers, and external customers) who were invited to discuss the work process with the workers.

Process Optimization

As soon as Evolution could see that the new vision had been internalized by staff, and after they had completed the company-wide process optimizations required by new government regulation, the staff was encouraged to begin optimizing their own work processes.

The Evolution of Evolution into a Learning Organization

The overall optimization task continued and even though there was intensive communication on this task, because not everyone could participate in this process, the TQM approach proved to have less impact than the cultural change approach. Consequently, the two approaches were combined into one—Evolution Textiles as a learning organization was born.

Process owners were trained to become the managers of their own work processes. Everyone could submit an improvement plan, although there was no obligation to do so. Depending on the budget and the necessary correlation with the corporate objectives, these plans were immediately implemented following consultation with at least one internal customer and the direct superior. Human resources and communication managers were kept informed to prevent some improvement projects from being swept under the rug.

The overall advantage of this combined TQM and culture change approach was that everyone was involved. Small, high-impact projects often had greater value in terms of communication impact and mentality change than major transformation projects.

External Communication in Support of the Internal Culture

The way in which the organization is considered from the outside looking in is a factor not to be underestimated for the company's internal image. The internal changes were also communicated externally, although not immediately. At a corporate level, customers and suppliers were informed of the results of all image surveys and of the steps that were taken. Where customers were involved in internal consultation sessions, they received a relevant debriefing. Since the customers were very interested in the development of the company, a corporate newsletter was drawn up for each segment and product range, and a new corporate video was made.

The external marketing communication was geared toward the mission of the company. To this end, the advertising agency received a new corporate briefing. The external communication was also updated, but more importantly, its performance was carefully measured.

Results

The outcome of all this activity was:

- The staff become owners within the policy—the staff are not taken by surprise
- The staff know what the desired behaviors and actions are
- Faster communication
- Help for staff in the assumption of any new task
- Greater customer satisfaction
- Improved operating results

DON'T BE OVERHASTY!

A change in the corporate culture cannot be achieved overnight. Indeed, even with the best communication support it will take at least a year before any visible result is achieved. A radical cultural change can only be effected over a period of perhaps three years. Much will depend on the skills, the emotions, and the potential of your people and the background of the company. Consequently, regular monitoring of the reactions of your people to the desired change should not be neglected. After all, as the leader, you are only the conductor of the orchestra and it is the people in the organization who are playing the instruments.

Why and When to Use an External Communications Advisor

The role of the communications adviser is that of a persuader, that is, to provide support, to formulate core messages more clearly, and to monitor processes. The communications advisor is, as it were, the conductor of the orchestra standing in the pit in front of the stage. In this role, the communications advisor must keep the management from lapsing into jargon or anecdotes because they don't want to be seen only as the bearers of bad news. The communications advisor must convince the management that they are in fact capable of coping with less positive messages. It is also up to the communication adviser to break down the fortress mentality, as it is essential that the staff have understanding of and insight into the job their colleagues have to do. Finally, it is his/her task to make it clear to the top management and line managers that their messages must harmonize with the evolution and vision of the company.

 Kaat L. Exterbille studied communications at the Erasmus University in Rotterdam, and at the Higher Institute for Business Education in Ghent. She also studied marketing management and business economics at the Institute of Post-University Management at the University of Antwerp and management policy at the Vlerick School of Management. She took various courses in advertising, direct marketing, culture audit, corporate communications, and management in Belgium and abroad.

Kaat started her career as advertising manager at the newspaper *Het Laatste Nieuws* (*The Latest News*). She switched to advertising and public relations agencies in Belgium and in the U.S. In May, 1990, she started Kate Thomas & Kleyn, corporate communications consultants together with Thomas & Kleyn International. In November, 1992, Kaat did a management buy-out and now fully owns Kate Thomas & Kleyn. Kaat has conducted several change programs and is able to guide her clients through their change processes both on a strategic and an operational level. The types of projects which Kate Thomas & Kleyn take on include: mergers and acquisitions, market re-positioning, quality projects, privatizations, internal restructuring, corporate culture reorientation, or market surveys. They have worked in the private and public sector organizations such as De Witte Lietaer, Heineken, the National Telephone Company, the National Electricity producers, the Belgian Railway, Traffic Services, and other large organizations.

REFERENCES

Deal, T. E., and Kennedy, A. A. *Corporate Cultures*. Reading, MA: Addison-Wesley Publishing Company, 1982.

Exterbille, K. "TQM Can Be DOA with Innovative Communication." *The Journal for Quality and Participation*, Vol. 19, No. 2, March 1996, pp. 32–35.

Hamilton, S. *A Communication Audit Handbook*. London: Pitman Publishing, 1987.

Httner, H., Renckstorf, K., and Wester, F. *Onderzoekstypen in de Communicatiewetenschap*. Houten/Diegem, Belgium: Bohn Stafleu Van Loghum, 1995.

Van der Erve, M. *Evolution Management: Winning in Tomorrow's Marketplace*. Oxford, U.K.: Butterworth-Heinemann, Ltd., 1994.

Van Hasselt, H. R. *Cultuurmanagement: Bedrijfscultuur en Veranderingsprocessen*. 's-Gravenhage, The Netherlands: Delwel, 1991.

Wool, C. K., and Glaser, J. E. "Learning Organization with Innovative Communication" (speech). IABC, 1994.

EDITOR'S NOTE:

When you don't have any particular destination in mind, any path or road will do, the joke goes. We laugh at such jokes, but don't feel much like laughing after months of failed effort when the only goal we had was: "We need quality to be competitive. So let's *do quality!*"

In the past few years, I've heard some people (they and their organizations shall not be named) say: "Quality? Been there, done that. We're doing . . . (fill in with an acronym or buzzword) now!" The not-so-subtle implication is that quality was something they plugged in or bought and no longer needed to pay any attention to.

It would take another book to cover how wrong that view is. It is sufficient to remember that the definition of quality is a target that moves with the expectations and perceptions of the very next customer. We should remind ourselves of the innovation cycle which says that not long after we introduce our new quality product or service, the customer begins to look first for small improvements and cost savings, then looks later for significant improvements; and finally expects us to reinvent it.

So, we finally get the notion that quality has to be created over and over again—it's a continuous process!

So now we know that continuous quality improvement of processes is needed. What's our first step? The second? Wait, there must be an overall sequence and a superstructure, no? Yes, there is.

Peter E. Beerten has taken both an architect's and a contractor's view to the continuous improvement process and mapped out for us the sequence and the macro–structure of continuous process improvement. With this macro view, I think you will have a better overall view of how to construct the basic structure. While we can't predict the details that will make your continuous improvement house work best for you, we can say that you can build it well with this macro-structure. And when you need to create a new continuous improvement process to serve the reinvented market you create a few years from now, it will serve you well again.

Chapter 5

Constructing a Flexible and Productive Organization Architecture for Continuous Improvement

Peter E. Beerten, Kate Thomas & Kleyn

In the era which is now fading fast, companies could count on proprietary technology and a hefty cash flow to protect their position in the market. In today's world this is no longer true. Reverse engineering can, it seems, be applied to any technology. Globalization of financing, and the advent of global takeover specialists have wiped out those advantages. Even the quality advantage which helped Japanese firms globalize themselves during the period from 1960 to 1980 can be duplicated quickly and has been by a number of emerging Asian manufacturers.

The only resource left that can give an organization the edge it needs to survive and thrive in turbulent times is the people they employ, their collective creativity, motivation, and productive potential. Executive officers around the globe are trying to fully engage and activate these hidden human resources. Although many have faltered in these efforts, the successes of those who have been able to construct flexible and productive human architectures have been notable. Worldwide, Xerox, Motorola, Honda, Toyota, Nissan, Sony, and others who have closely followed their lead are world leaders in their products and services.

Failure to succeed in creating a successful human architecture for high performance has most often been due to lagging or stop-and-go commitment to creating whole work systems based on a quality/service focus and achieved by involving the whole employee in both the design and implementation process.

It is clear now that to productively engage each employee one must involve them not only in the improvement but in the development of their work environment as well. This means that the executive officer needs to take all possible efforts to open the strategic vision/mission exercise to everyone in the company. This is not easy but it is a giant first step in answering the question of every employee from vice president to the inventory clerk who asks of the new process: "What's in it for me?"

The other basic error made by many who have not gotten the rewards they thought would come from quality and participation processes has been to try to *plug in* a process here and there, or lurch from one management fad to another in the hopes that one of them would take hold on its own. This produced much activity, a few results, and probably tripled the number of cynics. Plug–in business process re–engineering approaches, for example, which have relied on a group of experts *doing the thinking* for everyone else, have produced for many organizations disastrous unforeseen aftereffects.

In short, to activate the hidden creative part of your human resources, you need to include them in the future planning and development of the organization and to provide them with an efficient process improvement method to translate the objectives in tangible results.

When dealing in a productive way with change, one should not forget to improve and increase the communication between all levels and departments—a basis for every good working and functioning team during change and ongoing operations.

If we take the time and effort to construct first the three above-mentioned primary cornerstones, a participative vision/mission process, process management, and communication of our corporate architecture, then we will be able to create the foundation for a sound and lucrative corporate architecture.

WHERE TO START?

The ever-growing number of terms, concepts, and approaches is becoming quite a challenge for those of us attempting to advise our organizations on how to best implement and maintain quality and participation processes in our firms.

What do these phrases remind you of? "Who's on first, what's on second, and I don't know..." the old Abbott and Costello joke or a conversation about benchmarking, ISO 9000, re–engineering, preferred partnership, quality improvement teams, and so on? The questions that seem to come up in almost every conversation between two or more quality and participation practitioners any place on the planet are:

- Which methods, approaches, or techniques complement which?
- Which one is first or second?
- Which ones are used again and again during different phases of the improvement process?

I believe that the underlying question to all of these and related questions is this: Can we fit the different quality concepts together (chronologically and strategically) into a common framework—an architecture of quality and participation? The answer is, yes. Yes, we can create a quality and participation architecture from which we can build any number of quality and participation architectures customized to fit your firm's culture and market needs.

Time Sequence

Whenever I think about a total quality architecture, I see that there are clear links between the different quality concepts, and that any one of them leads to another. But what I also see is that the sequence may be adjusted by organizations according to their chosen strategies or circumstances. The quality and participation architecture which I will describe here is one based upon the most frequent and best known implementation strategy.

1. THE CORPORATE AND THE QUALITY AND PARTICIPATION VISION AND MISSION

The corporate mission (with its quality and participation mission included) is the capstone for all quality and participation architecture. Its design, look, and feel drives the design for the rest of the structure. If this capstone is designed and built without sufficient commitment by top management (demonstrated by their defining the core quality objectives and clearly tying these to the corporate vision and mission), it won't take long for the rest of the structure to weaken and fail.

While it is top management's responsibility and obligation to design the corporate vision and mission, all employees should be involved in developing the quality and participation mission. The quality and participation mission should be based upon extensive data collection and a clear understanding of the needs and interests of the firm's customers, employees, stockholders, suppliers, and appropriate community and/or government stakeholders in the organization's success.

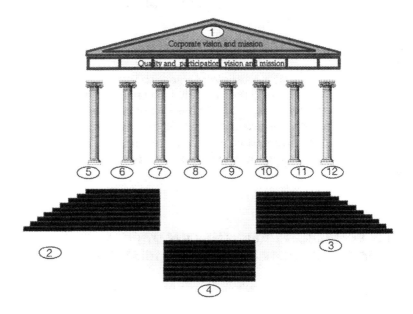

1. The corporate and quality and participation vision and mission
2. Corporate culture and style
3. The quality and participation technical and social Pareto analysis
4. Quality and participation process management
5. Corporate communications
6. Leadership
7. Customer surveys
8. Benchmarking
9. Re–engineering
10. Quality function deployment (QFD)
11. Preferred partnership
12. Business literacy

Figure 5.1 Creating an Architecture of Quality and Participation

Integrating the Corporate and the Quality and Participation Missions

If the corporate mission calls for increasing the firm's industrial market-share for its X, Y, and Z products by 8%, then the objectives of the quality and participation mission should call for optimizing and/or adapting its production/service processes to support gaining the desired goals for X, Y, and Z.

The danger of an inadequate or poorly formulated corporate mission is that the quality and participation mission will then also be inadequate or that the process will be viewed as an add–on, parallel process separate from the firm's general business objectives. If total quality and participation management isn't integrated into the everyday processes of the business, management's commitment to it will at best be a nice–to–do but not a have–to–do process. Even worse, it may be viewed as an initiative which hampers your ability to meet business objectives. In companies where this capstone has been integrated with the rest of the firm's architecture, we see managers who clearly see that the entire quality process supports meeting their business objectives in a more efficient manner and faster pace.

A production manager of a major brewing industry supplier in Belgium once told me: "I only began to believe in quality and participation when I finally saw the link between my productivity objectives (corporate mission) and my quality and participation projects—they helped me and my operators achieve a higher and higher quality output with our existing machinery."

2. CORPORATE CULTURE AND STYLE

Culture is at best a concept that is seen by many as having only to do with the arts and pleasures of society. Corporate culture is a confusing concept

---

The Flow from Corporate Vision to Evaluation Systems

Corporate vision
Corporate mission
Quality and participation mission
Corporate processes
Function and task descriptions
Evaluation systems

that is either discounted or taken lightly when implementing quality and participation. I can assure you that corporate culture has more meaning than this company plays Mozart in its lobby and another plays soft rock of the 1970s and 1980s.

When people say, "This approach doesn't seem to fit us, the way our people are," or, "it wasn't invented here," they are talking about maintaining the integrity of their corporate culture—that which makes them different from similar firms or organizations. Taking account of the specific make up of an organization's culture can be crucial in determining which, if any, type of quality and participation change process has a chance of succeeding or is doomed to failure. It is therefore important that those who are designing and implementing the quality and participation process to determine (through a deep slice of the organization) whether the organization has:

- A constructive culture with an emphasis on human values, good communications, initiative, and creativity
- A passive defensive culture which includes avoidance of responsibility, little initiative, and emphasis on rules and procedures
- An aggressive defensive one with internal divisions, power struggles, and negativism

Armed with this information, an organization can ask vital questions of itself, such as:

- Are we (the company) really ready to start a change process (quality and participation) using quality systems, even if we've already announced this in our corporate mission?
- Do we have management styles within our organizational culture which could disable or undermine a quality and participation process?
- How can we launch specific actions or exercises to finesse or neutralize any such negative styles?

There are a number of reliable exercises for such a test which provide both an audit and a point of departure for cultural readjustment.

3. THE QUALITY AND PARTICIPATION TECHNICAL AND SOCIAL PARETO ANALYSIS

During the introductory phase of a total quality management program (for baselining problem areas, as well as for awareness training), every employee should be consulted on existing problem areas in both the production/administrative (technical) and the supportive (social, internal communications, development) processes. The information from these surveys and/or interviews can then be displayed as Pareto diagrams which will give you a graphic, macro view of which work and administrative processes are in need of improvement and or redesign.

The Technical Pareto

With the technical Pareto in hand (and keeping the quality and participation mission in mind), top management can select technical improvement projects which support meeting the overall business objectives of the organization. Quite often, the focus will be on the ten most frequently mentioned technical (work process) problem areas and related costs of defects. These costs are usually identified by typical quality measurements (on time delivery, accuracy, efficiency, and productivity) and through appropriate interviews with employees directly involved with the work. The prospect of reducing defects costs can, in many cases, be used as a strong justification for a quality project and contribute to an active cost/return awareness among employees. Although not the only motivation for quality and participation, it is still a strong incentive for managers and executives to treat quality and participation as a potential cash cow and long–term benefit.

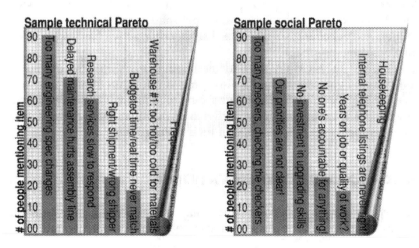

Following the large group awareness briefing on the firm's corporate mission and its quality and participation mission, comments are collected from those attending on what areas are in the greatest need of attention to help the organization meet its goals. These are then sorted into a technical and a social Pareto, enabling the company to prioritize which problem areas to attack first, second, and so on.

Figure 5.2   A Macro–Analysis of the Technical and Social Problem Areas

The Social Pareto

Management should now look at the social Pareto (social or administration problem areas) of the organization. This analysis can give a clear picture of how employees are dealing with:

- Collaboration within and between departments
- Management styles
- Distribution of information on policies
- Training and career possibilities

Project groups, in which management will be directly involved, can then work these issues according to the priorities derived from analysis of the social Pareto. This approach helps ensure that both management and operational levels see quality and participation as a process for improving the whole organization.

4. A SYSTEMATIC AND STRUCTURED APPROACH TO QUALITY AND PARTICIPATION PROCESS MANAGEMENT

Whether we are looking at a production or financial reporting system, this 12+ step process improvement model enables you to address directly both the technical and social issues listed earlier, as well as issues arising from customer feedback.

Using process language and methodology ensures that employees in different departments and levels can communicate clearly and freely over the Internet or intranet about their problem areas. The result is not only that their concerns will be understood, but that they will more easily win the support and cooperation of their colleagues.

5. CORPORATE COMMUNICATIONS

Quality thinking in a corporation not only calls for communications support in the introductory phase, but also needs to be explained and maintained throughout its subsequent development.

When we think about such corporate communications, many of us only think in terms of an expensive and colorful brochure. Corporate or internal communications is much more than that. In fact, it begins with a communications plan developed by the quality manager and in–house or external corporate communications specialists. The corporate quality communications plan should take into account the organization's culture and the targeted objectives of the overall quality and participation process, as well as specific projects.

All communications about improvement activities should be precisely timed and developed in conjunction with the relevant personnel so

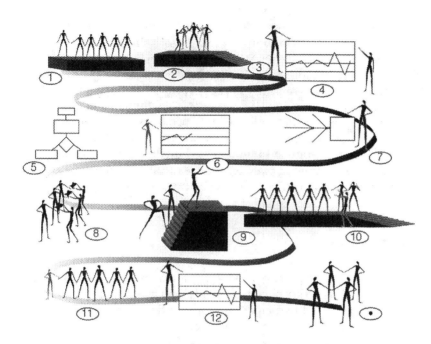

This process language and methodology ensures that employees in different departments and levels can communicate clearly and freely about their problem areas.
1. Gathering information from customers.
2. Reviewing customer policies and standards in light of new customer information.
3. Selecting and defining a process for an improvement project.
4. Measure the primary process.
5. Construct a flow diagram of the process.
6. Take intermediate process measurements.
7. Use a cause-and-effect (fishbone) diagram to aid in analysis of the problem.
8. Create and carry out a data collection strategy.
9. Analyze the data, conduct trial solutions, and select means to solve the process problem.
10. Present findings and proposed solution(s) to appropriate group(s).
11. Implement the improvement plan.
12. Measure and evaluate the improvements.
• When appropriate, institutionalize improvements organization wide (via ISO 9000, as well as other international or national quality, environmental, safety, and/or labor standards).

Figure 5.3 A 12+ Step Process Improvement Model

as to result in a series of carefully judged and effective projects involving various groups of employees (departments and hierarchy).

The quality communications plan should not only result in a clear and well-presented brochure, but also in a broader arsenal of management speeches, round tables with management, introductory presentations, video news, and newsletters.

Choosing the right media to suit the culture of the company is very important. It is essential that this communications process operate steadily and keep all employees regularly and clearly informed on all matters relating to quality and participation.

In large as well as medium–size enterprises (100 persons and above) a well-elaborated communications policy is anything but a superfluous luxury. It is a system that will prevent specific departments or people being cut off from quality and participation and other strategic information. A well-thought-out and implemented quality communications plan will go a long way toward overcoming the traditional hoarding of information as the means to gain and retain corporate power and status.

6. LEADERSHIP

The communications process just described cannot be thought of as a substitute for direct and personal quality and participation leadership. The global quality and participation project and all quality and participation improvement projects need to be clearly led. All too often this is what is lacking and not leading is the first fatal error to obtaining a successful and effective quality and participation process. The worst sign that leadership is inadequate, shows when in the name of participation, someone is asked to lead a process without sufficient preparation or training. We know that most people are not born leaders, but we also know that the relevant skills can be learned.

Improving an Organization's Leadership Capacity

The first step in improving an organization's leadership capacity is to identify people's leadership potential by assessing your organization for its collective skills in:

- Listening and communication
- Setting objectives
- Delegation and coaching
- Team development
- Participative management
- Recognition

Once such an assessment is done, you can concretely identify development needs and resources. Even though there are a number of relevant evaluation and counseling programs in existence, managers should be ready to give their own generous attention to these matters, in their interest and in the interest of their employees who are the next generation of company leaders.

Too many organizations pay little attention to developing leadership at all levels of their organizations and end up paying for it in low morale and lost customers awaiting decisions that could have been made at the contact level, as well as organization crisis when a group of leaders retires without competent replacements.

I often notice that individual planning or development systems are missing in some or all departments of organizations having difficulty in producing consistent customer satisfying products or services. When leadership capacity is assessed and a leadership development improvement plan implemented effectively, it can lead to a genuine breakthrough in both collaboration and productivity.

7. CUSTOMER SURVEYS

Many organizations who do any customer analysis go directly and only to the external customer to get an idea of which products and services are in need of optimization. Those with a more complete view prefer to develop a Pareto analysis together with their internal customers (employees) and tidy up their own front yard before they address the customer.

After a running–in period during which one has to deal primarily with cleaning up internal processes, you should consult with the external customer to find out to what extent he/she is satisfied with the changes made and whether he/she has any specific expectations with regard to process improvements.

This should be done carefully so as not to create false expectations and to enable you to make clear agreements on specific improvements and how the customer might make a positive contribution to those improvements. If you and your company are new at tapping internal and external customer information, you should seek competent outside assistance, designed for growing your capacity to conduct your own customer data collection and analysis.

Conducting both internal and external customer surveys regularly will help you elaborate upon and improve your existing technical and social Pareto analysis substantially—such measurement is not a one shot or a once in a while process.

8. BENCHMARKING

Internal Benchmarking

With the first successful internal quality and participation projects completed, there will be a lot of interest in creating an internal benchmark or reference point for optimal working processes. Many companies that adopt this kind of exercise send the concerned employees out to exchange experiences/knowhow with their colleagues involved in the same working process.

External Benchmarking

In some cases research companies are brought in to determine, for example; within a clearly defined market segment, how many corrections/errors in the invoicing process are generated on average in a month, or what is the average time it takes a production unit to complete a specific process.

When establishing or using external benchmarks, we have to be quite clear about which processes we are comparing and which colleagues we can and wish to get into a clinch with. The poor results of comparing apples with pears has led a lot of companies to opt for the more easily controlled and more manageable internal benchmark.

Although independent benchmarking committees and even departments have been set up in a lot of companies, the quality manager or organization manager is the best placed person to initiate this type of operation and to communicate the data and results. His or her understanding of process management will give better insight into the right choice of benchmark projects.

Finally, we should not forget that benchmarking is not a panacea or substitute for weeding first in your own garden. Managers need to choose very carefully between the different benchmarks available to arrive at a small number which offer a tangible benefit to the organization and can be put into effect with little or no risk (cost/return).

9. RE-ENGINEERING

Re–engineering is sometimes presented as a discrete improvement discipline or philosophy, something that we also find with benchmarking, preferred partnership, and quality function deployment. It is only a part of total quality management and should be seen as a continuation of the process management state of mind. Many quality and participation workgroups combine improvement measures with the re–engineering or reorganization of their work process, in line with the corporate mission.

Who Should Be Involved in Redesign?

Regardless of whether you are thinking of using the recently popularized re–engineering processes, work redesign, socio–technical analysis, or a combination of the search conference followed by a participative design workshop, it is absolutely vital that the process owners are intimately involved in the structural and functional reorganization process of their work.

Even when you use external market surveys and experience to determine that specific products and services need to be adapted or completely remodeled, the employees directly involved in the process are still the best placed people to participate in the process restructuring task.

Some companies are too quick to call on the services of external consultants when they could in fact mobilize their own system and employees (internal redesign teams). Managers who hesitate to use their own people in even the most modest re–engineering projects risk not only getting the wrong answers, but taking longer to reorganize the work.

Think Twice Before Re–engineering Even Once

Too often the cry of those who haven't taken the time to understand their existing system of work processes is: "Let's reorganize! Let's re–engineer!" Re–engineering or restructuring should only be undertaken in a systemic way and based upon external and internal facts which clearly point a need to reorganize work processes.

10. QUALITY FUNCTION DEPLOYMENT

At its core, quality function deployment (QFD) is a method for bringing the customer into both the design process and the improvement process. The customer's product or service expectations and needs can be translated into a matrix of product/service specifications. This matrix can then be used to compare existing product or service characteristics to those outlined by the customer.

If you complete a similar matrix for directly competing products or services (derived from benchmarking), these two matrices can then be combined and assessed in terms of the potential added value of different product/service characteristics.

When, on the basis of concrete customer data, an organization decides to adapt its production processes, then, as when integrating a benchmark, you should use a process improvement model as previously shown. Using the improvement model is relevant because the work process is being partly or entirely reorganized and, as a result, some process owners are being partly or fully confronted with new tasks, functions, or responsibilities.

11. PREFERRED PARTNERSHIP

Preferred partnership seems to be one of the most misunderstood concepts in Total Quality Management. The simplest definition of a preferred partnership is this: *A preferred partnership is a management and cooperation system for the company and all its possible suppliers. It fosters a proactive exchange of product and service data between the organization and its suppliers.*

The Link between Data and Trust

This exchange starts with the task of bringing jointly produced products and services up to a projected quality standard and keeping them there.

Here, in addition to quality evaluation or audit (ISO 9000, Baldrige, or EFQM), which is only a snapshot of the entire concept, suppliers receive information and support in setting up a process management system. At this level both partners work toward a mutually acceptable system where a maximum of data is exchanged.

The Hard Second Step

Once both parties feel they have a solid relationship built on trust, the second step is to work together on the joint development of products or services in line with quality and participation principles. This implies that the company and its suppliers will exchange data within the context of a clearly defined assignment to develop a new product or service. Obviously, it's not that easy reaching the second level. In fact, many companies have approached this process simply as a means to reduce the number of suppliers and/or as a means to exert more control over the few remaining suppliers. In the long run, a slash-and-burn approach to suppliers is an increasingly untenable situation—there are simply too many competitors lurking about in the world looking for high quality and reliable partners. Finally, the expectations and motivation of suppliers go much further than slavish submission to, and compliance with, a first–generation quality control system.

12. BUSINESS LITERACY

If you are convinced of the importance and the role the process owners play in Total Quality Management, then you have every reason to lay open company policy and performance data to them.

Motivational studies in recent years have clearly shown that employees place considerable importance on knowing about company policy and related communications. "You hardly belong until you are really familiar with and a part of the company's objectives" is a sentiment that can often be heard at operational level.

It is essential that company managers be properly prepared and active in this area. If management fails to invest time to elaborate company objectives clearly and then communicate these appropriately to all process owners, it takes the risk of creating a vacuum which draws into it rumors, apathy, and dangerous assumptions, and produces consequent losses in productivity.

When employees have information that enables them to translate stated company objectives (volume, profit, ROI, ROA) into their daily work, they can align their individual goals to meet those same objectives. In addition, employees feel a greater readiness to be evaluated in accordance with the same, and now fully accepted, objectives.

An evaluation system based on full business literacy by all employees should also be one which is elaborated and accepted by both parties. It should be clearly designed to assess (not condemn) the employee on the basis of measurable concepts linked with the general and equally measurable company objectives. In this way, people are informed and interested not only in their personal performance but also in the company's annual results.

FINAL THOUGHTS

Building the future begins with dreams, visions, and hopes, to be sure. But creating a desirable future also takes both a disciplined view of the steps which must be taken to get there and which comes first, second, and so on. Unless it is a solitary future you are building, those who will contribute to creating that future must have both an effective voice based on knowledge and involvement in what that future will be and the right tools (training, work structure, resources, and data) in heads, hearts, and hands.

Peter E. Beerten is a managing director of the Kate Thomas & Kleyn (KT&K, located in metro-Brussels). KT&K specializes in TQM architecture and related human resource and communications systems. Prior to becoming a consultant to business firms such as Heineken, Uncle Ben's, Campbell Soup, Mars, and BP Chemicals, Beerten gained hands–on organizational experience with Massport International in Boston, Massachusetts, the Terumo Corporation in Tokyo, Japan, and Puratos in Brussels, Belgium. Beerten has served as a guest lecturer at the Catholic University of Leuven, Belgium and as a member of the executive committee of the Belgian Center for Total Quality Management.

Part 2

Additional Tools and Approaches

Chapter 6

Our Customers Expect
Total Transaction Quality

John Guaspari, Rath & Strong

> If an award were given for the business topic about which the most has
> been written in recent memory: non-Donald-Trump-division the hands-
> down winner would have to be "quality and the automobile industry."

We've all read the data comparing the defects-per-thousand vehicles
of the U.S. and Japanese car fleets. We've all read the claims about safety,
reliability, and repair rates. We've all read stories describing the performance of American factories run by Japanese management and American
factories run by American management. (We haven't read about Japanese
factories run by American management. That's because "the playing field
isn't level," which we have read about.)

There is no question that all of those things are very interesting and
important. Nor is there any question that by many quality criteria, things
have gotten significantly better. But having recently gone through the experience of buying a new—and for the record, American—car, I was once
again reminded of just how much room for improvement there still is.

Opportunities abound and they have nothing to do with the quality
of the product or the quality of the service department. They have instead
to do with the quality of the overall car-buying experience, an experience
filled with enough ritual behavior to keep budding cultural anthropolo-
gists in dissertation material for generations.

BUYING A CAR IN AMERICA

You know the drill. Having decided that you are formally in the market
for a new car, you enter the showroom. A salesman (it is almost invariably
a salesman) swoops down upon you and after some boilerplate chitchat,
asks, "What will it take to put you in a new car today?" You look him

straight in the eye, summon up a look of absolute righteousness, and lie through your teeth. He looks surprised (a lie) at your response and tells you that the already marked down price is about as far as they can go (a lie). You respond that there's no way you can afford any more than you have already offered (a lie). He says that if it were up to him, he'd be glad to sell it to you at that price (a lie), but it's the sales manager's call, and although he doubts the sales manager will budge off the price (a lie), he'll go talk to him and see what he can do. Round and round it goes until all interested parties are exhausted by this orgy of prevarication and a deal is struck. Car keys, registrations, and thousands of dollars change hands, and you leave the showroom, pleased with your new car, but feeling vaguely as though you need a bath.

> Assertion: For the vast majority of us, the experience of buying a car is a singularly unpleasant one.

If people in the car business would spend just a small fraction of the time worrying about that reality than they do fulminating about x-year, x-mile warranties, and how American made cars are just as good as you know whose, they would sell more cars. That might seem obvious, and it is when you are looking at things from a customer's perspective.

BUYING THE WHOLE EXPERIENCE— TOTAL TRANSACTION QUALITY

Things quickly become a lot less apparent, though, when we find ourselves in the middle of the complex processes by which our customers have the experience of doing business with us—when we're on the job. This isn't because we don't care how our customers are treated. (I don't really think that people in the car business intend for us to feel so put off by the car-buying experience.) It's a matter of focus.

Quality Focus #1

The ultimate objective of a total quality effort is not to produce defect-free products or to deliver flawless service, but to *create happy customers*. To be sure, quality products and service are important, but they should be seen as the means to the end and not the end in itself.

Quality Focus #2

The package within which we either do or do not deliver that customer happiness is the total experience of doing business with us—*the total transaction*. Therefore, from an operating point of view, our attention ought to be on total transaction quality. Adopting this focus can be the first step toward creating customers who are not just happy, but downright delighted to do business with us.

Many businesses do not operate that way. Instead, departments, functions, and individuals worry about their private corners of the world. Then, through a communal leap of faith that makes Michael Jordan seem positively earthbound, it is assumed that things will come together at the customer. Or if things go wrong, service will take care of it. Or the waitress. Or the nurse. Or the poor soul who happens to pick up the phone when the unhappy customer calls.

True Story

I wrote this portion of this article on a flight from Los Angeles to Boston. Three hours ago, I stopped in an airport coffee shop for breakfast. A number 3, on the menu board behind the short-order cook consisted of scrambled eggs, bacon or sausage, hash browns, and biscuits. The price: $4.95. The guy in front of me ordered a number 3. The cook told him that they were out of biscuits. The guy in front of me asked what the price would be without the biscuits. The cook said she would have to ask the manager. Thirty seconds later the manager appeared out front. "What's a number 3 cost without the biscuits?" she asked. "Same price as with them," answered the manager, who then went back through the doors, out of sight, apparently to tend to some *important manager stuff.* The guy in front of me laughed (this is not the kind of delight I was talking about above), shook his head, and walked away. The short-order cook turned to a co-worker and said, "They leave us here to deal with the customers. They don't see it." Exactly!

Reverse Engineer the Transaction

So how do you build a quality transaction that will lead to happy customers? You get your hands on a sampling of transactions and systematically take them apart to see how they were built. You reverse engineer the transaction. As an example, let's consider the business of putting on seminars. I've chosen the seminar business both because it's a business I've had experience in, and, far more important, virtually everyone reading this article has attended seminars, delivered seminars, or both.

Analyzing the Total Transaction

The end product of our quality efforts, the total transaction, appears on the far right of Figure 6.1 Inside the far right box appears the single most important element in this entire process: a concise statement of what the customer feels after having received a quality transaction written from the point of view of the customer.

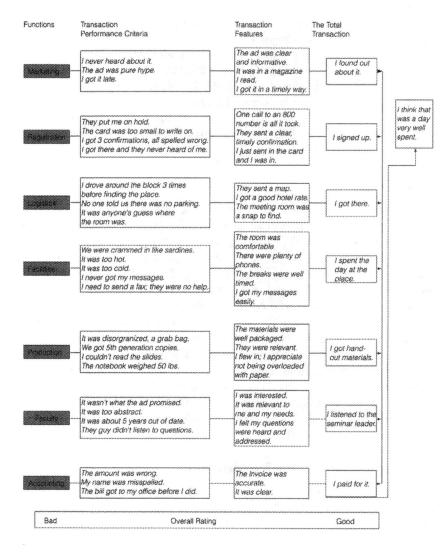

Figure 6.1   Total Transaction Quality

For our seminar example, such a statement might be: "I think that was a day very well spent." If you're in the computer industry, the following might appear in the total transaction box: "Trying to keep up with what's available in the computer field is mind boggling. I'm confident my needs will be taken care of by my supplier." Someone in the hotel business might write: "I'm after a pleasant, hassle-free environment while I'm on the road."

I cannot emphasize enough the importance of framing these statements in the customer's words. They should be "I" statements—it is people we are selling to, not account numbers. They should be in quotation marks; it's not how we'd say it, but how our customers might say it. And they should be broad, impressionistic statements. We might like to assume our customers rate our performance based on a rigorous analysis of the complex equations which describe the elegant processes by which we carry out work in our organizations, but we will have made better assumptions in our lives.

Transaction Features   Moving left in this figure, we come to a column headed Transaction Features. These are the activities a customer must go through when doing business with us. (As you move down the page, you should be moving forward in time.) Once again, this set of statements should be "I" statements and they should be in quotes.

Transaction feature statements for the computer customer might include, "I worked with them to configure the system," and "I bought a service contract." In the hotel business, statements like "I ordered from room service," and "I used the express checkout service" might be appropriate.

Keep the language colloquial   The seminar business' catalog might tell its customers that they "will be immersed in an enriching bath of cutting edge concepts, sharing insights and ideas with forward thinking peers amidst all that the state of the art in educational settings has to offer," but they're more likely to say, "I spent the day at the place."

Transaction Performance Criteria   Move left one more column in the figure and you'll find the heading Transaction Performance Criteria. Once again there are statements written from the customer's point of view, and once again they are quotes. But where the statements under Transaction Features are intentionally value-neutral, these are anything but. They range from Bad at the left ("I got three confirmations, all spelled wrong.") to Good at the right ("One phone call to an 800 number and I was in."). There should be numerous statements here because whether they realize it or not, your customers are rating you on many, many performance criteria, and this is the place to identify as many of them as possible.

The very act of filling in this portion of the diagram—peeling back one more level of detail in the reverse engineering process—is an important step in sensitizing an organization to "what it's really like to do business with us."

Overall Rating   Again note that as you move down the page, you are also moving forward in time. It stands to reason that at the bottom of this column there is a scale labeled Overall Rating. (It should also stand to reason that this rating is linked directly to the customer's impression of the Total Transaction: "That was a day well spent."

It's important to note that it is much easier to move from right to left as you move down the page (to go from a good rating to a bad rating as you move forward in time) than it is to go from left to right. For example, if the seminar room was poorly ventilated so that our customer was physically uncomfortable, she is less likely to be impressed by the whiz bang graphics on our slides. And while we may have done a first-rate job by all other criteria, if we mess up the billing and force our customer through a lot of hoops to get things straightened out, he's not likely to come back again. Three key summary points to a total transaction quality analysis are:

1. It is a many-dimensional matter.
2. Everything matters.
3. Right to left is easier than left to right.

The Transaction Has Been Reverse Engineered: Now What?

Now that we've torn the total transaction apart and have all of the component pieces neatly organized, what can we learn from it? What characterizes an organization which regularly builds quality transactions from one which doesn't?

Most of us don't have the luxury of building a greenfield transaction factory. We already have an organization in place. Move left from the Transaction Performance Criteria column. The first thing you'll hit is a wall representing the barrier, both literal and figurative, between your business and your customers. Go a little further left and you'll see a column headed Functions which represent the various production areas of our transaction factory.

In our example, the functions might be marketing, registration, logistics, facilities, production, faculty, and accounting. Notice that these functions line up one for one with the Transaction Performance Criteria and therefore, the Transaction Features. Having now noticed that, you might be saying to yourself, "Our organization is more complex than that. Things don't line up quite that nicely for us." The issue, however, isn't whether they do line up that way. It's whether they should. It's not an easy matter to produce and deliver and support quality transactions. If your organizational structure adds several layers of complexity to the task, then it is a part of the problem.

John Guaspari is author of *I Know It When I See It, Theory Why,* and *The Customer Connection: Quality for the Rest of Us.* His message has also been translated into three training program videotapes: *I Know It When I see It, Why Quality,* and *The Quality Connection* (AMA Film Video). He is a popular speaker and has been a board of directors member for the AQP. This article first appeared in the September, 1990 issue of *The Journal for Quality and Participation.*

Chapter 7

The Power of Community Search Conferences

Merrelyn Emery, Australian National University

Australia 1995 is a very different place from what it was in 1972. The reasons go far beyond its film and recording stars—the use of community search conferences has played a significant role in changing the face of Australia.

Since 1972, people have created new organizations to deal with issues arising from the continuous process of change itself. They have directly created new national policies and directions. The search conference has touched and changed a huge diversity of geographical communities, industries, and institutions across the country. And we are talking about thousands of searches.

Apart from these direct effects, there has been an indirect but perhaps even more important cumulative effect: The great mass of energy involved and created during these search conferences has also been directed toward creating environments that are supportive of community based on our highest human ideals. The basic set of ideals which the search conference elicits provides direction and a powerful sense of democratic community.

PLANNING AND WORK WITHIN PARTICIPATIVE DEMOCRATIC COMMUNITIES

Democratic communities take responsibility for their future. Within them individuals grow as the communities develop responsible, democratic, and cooperative ways. It is undeniable that cohesive community events based on ideals create a sense of community. The excitement and joy that people feel when they work together for their community and future means that they will attempt to recreate that experience. It becomes their preferred way. It is easily arguable on the basis of these thousands of community search conferences that Australia's modern day success as a multi-cultural nation has its origins in the strong sense of community and tolerance that search conferences have both nurtured and created.

THE LIFE OF THE NATION
BEGINS IN THE LOCAL COMMUNITY

Is Australia heaven on earth? No. Of course not. It's still basically a representative democracy. And it is impossible to track all lines of influence through time in any unit as big as a diverse nation. But there is a clear line of development within Australia, that of community revitalization. No democratic community or nation can survive without an infrastructure of strong cohesive communities. While the search conference in Australia has not created New Utopia, it has encouraged an understanding, a continuing potential for working together for the common good.

SO WHAT IS A
COMMUNITY SEARCH CONFERENCE?

A community search conference is a carefully planned event in which a community plans its own future and takes responsibility for making it happen. The community may be geographical such as a town or a region. It may be a community of interest brought together by the need to plan for an industry or a policy area.

The Basic Concept or Design Principle Is Simple

The basic concept of a community search conference is that responsibility is located with the people who have to live with the consequences of their actions and the plan. Experts who fly in and out cannot do it by definition. As the Gungahlin kids realized, community means nothing if people have no control of their physical and social environment.

The Design

Community searches usually follow the simple classical design of exploring the external social environment, the system that is the town, industry, or issue and then integrating these into a set of strategies and detailed action plans to achieve their most desirable future.

> Changes in the world around us
> Probable and desirable futures of our town

Common history of our town
Our current town: what to keep, throw-out, create
Desirable future of our town
Action planning
Diffusion to the community
Implementing the plan

Differences between an Organizational and a Community Search

Community searches differ from organizational or corporate searches in three major ways.

1. Asking the Right Questions. A community search conference usually involves more preparation and planning than organizational search conferences. Communities usually:

- Are more diffuse with no definite internal structure.
- Have more diverse and complex sets of relationships, people, and interests than corporations.
- Often have a range of presenting symptoms: some people will focus on youth unemployment, others on environmental degradation, and some will see economic development opportunities as conflicting with environmental and cultural sustainability.

Everybody knows that things must change but how? Pre-work involves bringing all these views together and sometimes results in totally redefining the focus of the search conference. In small discrete areas, for example, the most productive focus is usually simply *the future of our town.* But getting it right takes time. *Be prepared.*

2. Having All Pieces of the Puzzle in the Room The selection of participants for a community search conference is absolutely critical to its success. For organizational search conferences, there is little if any decision making about participants. The corporate strategic plan is the responsibility of top management or the board of directors and these attend the search. The community search, on the other hand, must involve a process of researching the nature of the community, drawing up a *social map* and using that map as the basis of the *community reference system.* The community reference system ensures that the community itself determines who attends. It also ensures that the participants collectively know all the pieces of the puzzle involved in the future of that community.

In many issue search conferences, there is a great deal of work to be done in identifying all the pieces of the puzzle and the people who hold the relevant knowledge about those pieces. For The Future of Australia's Marginal Lands (1980), key organizations and individuals in every state were visited. "Selecting three dozen participants from a list of over 200 was not easy," but many participants wore two or more relevant hats. The diversity was huge—lawyers, farmers and graziers, environmental scientists, parliamentarians, a welfare project officer, public servants, a wool manager, and others. All states and sectors were there. And the puzzle was in the room.

3. Making It Happen   In most community searches, there is no existing structure to implement the ensuing plan.[1] This has long been a major reason for the ultimate failure of many community search conferences. Our cultural brainwashing and tradition has led us to believe that we should set up committees to do everything and anything. But committees are, for the most part, only mini-bureaucracies and their dynamics and outcomes follow suit. Such committees create endless fight/flight, inertia, and low quality outcomes, if any. The low energy and negative emotions associated with committees are the opposite of what people have experienced in the search conference itself. They quickly give up on the process and it dies. Democratic structures must, therefore, be created.

Today, we build in a component at the end of the search to overcome this difficulty. We build in a modified participative design workshop to design an organizational structure to carry out the implementation in a democratic way. Once the concepts and practices of democracy through self-management are understood and participants have designed their own structure, the community has a much better chance of making its most desirable future happen. Not only has it come alive, it has consciously learned how to organize itself for an effective, long-term, and adaptive life. When the environment changes again as it will, the community has the tools, not only to adjust its plans but also to reorganize itself.

1972–1977: OUR COMMUNITIES COME ALIVE

Kids Show Planners the Future

At the beginning of the Canberra winter of 1973, 34 people, aged between 16 and 25, went up the mountains to plan Gungahlin, a new town of Canberra, the decentralized (bush) national capital of Australia. In the process, they destroyed myths and created others. *The professional planners*

---

[1] In organizational search conferences and some industry search conferences where there is a pre-existing industry association, implementation is naturally coordinated by that body in cooperation with the search conference membership.

didn't think the kids could plan. The National Capital Development Commission (NCDC), responsible for the planning of Canberra made every possible contingency plan against how they assumed Murphy's law would work in our search conference. And despite our best efforts, Angela Sands and I could not overcome their skepticism about this age group's abilities to work or to self manage. The search was therefore scheduled for five days and a leader was assigned to three predetermined subgroups. (The NCDC also didn't believe they could plan.) The NCDC brought masses of technical information and expert planners. (Neither was called upon during the search.) Worse than this, with the usual protective and paternalistic concern, no night work had been scheduled. It had even been suggested that the kids might not work through a whole day. But then the staff couldn't stop them working and couldn't get them to bed!

Their Community, Gungahlin, was Years Ahead of Its Time

Angela Sands, the co-search manager, said in 1975, the memories are of "immense energy and enthusiasm." They were committed to finding idealistic and realistic solutions. They planned a SHE town, what James Robertson was later to describe as the "sane, humane, and ecological" alternative. News of it spread rapidly. Professional planners took a deep breath.

Then They Wanted to Keep on Meeting

Not only had they planned a community, they had become one! As Angela evaluated it a year later, the search conference had delivered on its promises and the ideals were evident. Many of the ideas were immediately incorporated into other parts of Canberra's development. The NCDC then took the plans forward into the structural planning phase. Gungahlin is now being built. Some of the original vision is included as the conventional wisdom it has now become. Two other search conferences were sponsored by the NCDC for the future of Canberra and the future of Belconnen, another newly established town. They confirmed the ideals and values evident in the first. The Gungahlin kids had made history.

Alternatives to Freeways

During 1974, traffic studies for Geelong predicted that by 1991, there would be a road and traffic crisis. (Geelong is a small city in the south of Victoria which was then growing rapidly.) A world-renowned civil engineering consultancy firm was brought in to plan a solution for the throughway from Melbourne to the beaches on the South Coast. Their recommendation: a six-lane freeway which would split the city into two and destroy many houses. Most residents opposed the plan and an environmental and social impact study was ordered. We were asked whether one of these new-fangled search conferences could help. Again, we wrestled not only with the Geelong Regional Planning Authority, but also with the other social planners who had been contracted to look after aspects of the job.

The Search for Alternatives   The ensuing search conference was highly creative. Its participants evaluated all the available options and created some of their own. As the final report noted, they were strongly attached to the character of Geelong as a town rather than a city and worked to preserve this character. No outside body could possibly do that. A final plan was developed based upon a stretch of freeway outside the town plus designing and upgrading traffic management conditions within it. It allowed for adaptive, step-by-step implementation as traffic volumes increased. To this day, there is no freeway running through the center of Geelong and no need for one either.

The Beginning of the Community Reference System   It was for Geelong that we devised the *community reference system* to ensure that we had a non-biased selection of the population.

It worked well as a subsequent community survey proved. But we made one mistake. We assumed that we could define Geelong by drawing a circle around the city. The participants disagreed. They drew their own boundary which was far from circular and worked on their definition. This enabled them to see options nobody had dreamt of. Again, the news travelled fast. Nobody had seen 30 ordinary citizens behaving like that before.

The Emergence of a New Planning Paradigm   If the planning of Gungahlin had put many social planners and community development officers on red alert, Geelong confirmed that remote expert planners were gone. The new role for planners had to be a partnership with the community.

The Community Reference System Is Used for Selecting Participants in a Community Search Conference

The community determines its own members whether it is a geopolitical, professional, or issue-related community. There are seven distinct steps to locating individuals to include in the search conference:

1. Research a rough social map.
2. Decide on relevant criteria:

   Known to be actively concerned about X.
   Other as relevant to X.

3. Pick a starting point in each section of the map.

4. Ask each starting point for two or three names that fit the criteria.

5. Ask each of the new names to give you two or three names that fit the criteria.

6. After one, two, or three iterations, the same names should appear.

7. Select from the total list (cover the total map—jigsaw puzzle).

As can be seen in this hypothetical social map, many different groups, sectors, and interests, each of which are considered a part of the

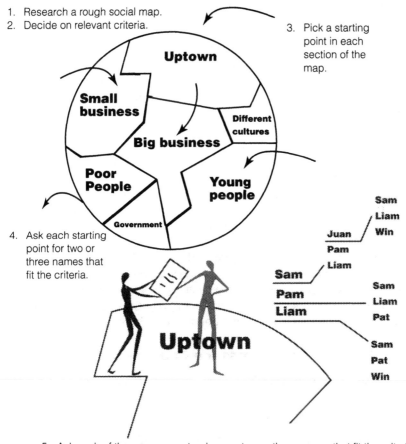

1. Research a rough social map.
2. Decide on relevant criteria.

3. Pick a starting point in each section of the map.

Uptown

Small business

Different cultures

Big business

Poor People

Young people

Government

4. Ask each starting point for two or three names that fit the criteria.

Uptown

Sam
Liam
Win

Juan
Pam

Sam
Liam

Sam
Pam
Liam

Liam

Sam
Liam
Pat

Sam
Pat
Win

5. Ask each of the new names to give you two or three names that fit the criteria.
6. After one, two, or three iterations, the same names should appear.
7. Select from the total list (cover the total map—jigsaw puzzle).

Figure 7.1   The Community Reference System

system as defined by the community, may be included in a particular community search.

THE SEARCH CONFERENCE GROWS IN SCOPE AND APPLICATION

Some planning subjects and areas were so large and decentralized that more than one search conference was required. A series of searches became a common means to planning regional development or the development of specific aspects or facilities within regions and across the country.

Freemantle Defends the America's Cup

In 1983, Australia won the America's Cup and the venue chosen for its next defense was the city of Freemantle in Western Australia. The city, a neighbor of Perth, was at the time a working class community not equipped to meet the needs of a world class sporting event with all its attendant spectators and media. The story of how Freemantle successfully hosted the event begins in 1977 when 12 search conferences were held in key centers of a huge region of Western Australia. They focused on the development of community recreation facilities. As communities were energized, the conferences evolved over time. By 1983, the city had held six search conferences. These conferences provided the framework for the redevelopment of the city for the defense of the Cup.

Instead of tearing out the heart of the cities as other cities around the world had done to host world class events, the city's experience with building values into its planning through its previous searches enabled it to retain its character and be a world class host for the America's Cup. These included access to the river by all, provision of low-cost housing, preservation of historic areas, and redevelopments limited to three stories high. Freeo, as we call it, is now an open and exciting city, acclaimed by all.

Search Conferences Across the Country

During this same period right across the country, the search conference blossomed in both scope and depth:

- Preschool kids were designing their own playgrounds.
- University classes were introduced to and run by the principles of the search.
- The leisure clubs in New South Wales began to plan their future as community clubs through a long series of searches.

- A national group planned for telecommunications in 2000. A countless number of such searches have been held since then in different regions and aspects of Telecom's operations.
- A new maximum security prison was designed on site in a prison—an inmate escaped during the event.
- Nurses planned their future through education. They are now a highly educated profession.
- Some focused on youth, some on the elderly. And the search conference began to be used by corporations.

It Was Truly a Time of Great Excitement

The search conference was showing people that the future was truly theirs to make. It allowed communities to translate their new perspectives into effective action. The old expert-driven and top-down methods of making change were effectively dead. Task-oriented work by communities making their own plans and implementing them became the way to go. Responsibility for communities, their own affairs and lives in cooperation with others, and the larger representative structures was being relocated with the communities themselves. The testing was extensive. We realized we had a powerful tool in our hands. Much of the learning was collected together for a search on the search: *Searching, 1982.* But there was more to come before this tool could reliably deliver sustainable communities. This accumulated new learning can be found in *Searching, 1996.*

THE SEARCH CONFERENCE AND NATIONAL POLICIES

These examples also form an evolving series, although they were not designed that way. Together they illustrate one of the powers of community search conferences, namely, that the forces they create to spread the message and the method, create an ever increasing momentum that eventually becomes irresistible. And then things happen!

Industrial Relations Summit: 1973

The group that attended the first Industrial Relations Summit in 1973 was as far from being a community as it was possible to be. Industrial relations across the land were atrocious. The country was wracked by strikes and there was open warfare between unions and management. Similar struggles were taking place within the union movement itself and between employer bodies. There was an activist national labor government and rapid social change—a volatile mix.

The search conference was initiated by the Centre for Continuing Education of the Australian National University to bring together key people able to influence the present and future shape of national industrial relations on a personal rather than a representative basis. The 30 participants covered major areas of the industrial relations scene and were joined by key people from government and academia. Because of the conflicted context, its planning and organizing became a marathon, a trial of endurance.

Once the search was underway, however, it became clear that the agreements heavily outweighed the disagreements. They agreed:

- About the major factors influencing change in the broad social environment.
- That moving from bureaucratic to democratic workplaces was a core solution for the future.
- About the necessity for the education of management about this shift.
- That industrial relations in the future would place more emphasis on *future building* rather than narrow and short term negotiations.

In short, they proved to each other that their jointly held expectations that each of them held widely divergent views were wrong.

Results   They explored the future world of work in detail and reaffirmed the centrality of democratic structures for quality work for all. Their strategies were comprehensive and again agreed. They gave unanimous advice to government. They recommended more future searches with an enlarged membership, and planned the next. From its difficult pregnancy and labor, this child had become a prodigy within two days and two nights. It too had become a community.

National Manufacturing Policy: 1975   In 1974 the Prime Minister appointed a high-powered committee, drawn from the private and public sectors and academia, to devise appropriate policies for the development of manufacturing industry. It was chaired by Gordon Jackson, CEO of CSR Ltd., one of Australia's biggest companies and of course, it became known as the Jackson Committee. The committee assembled a similarly high-powered and broad-based supporting secretariat. It was agreed that they should produce a discussion paper and take a broad approach to manufacturing, including social and regional issues as well as economic.

The Search Conference Rescues a Committee that Couldn't Get Off the Start Line   They began life as a committee and, as should be expected, found it difficult to pull together all the diverse views and facts they faced. Knowing of the search conference, the chairman approached Fred Emery and asked him to help. Fred and I ran a search conference during which they integrated their work into an agreed and consistent set of policies:

1. By understanding the environment in which industry would have to operate, and by understanding the forces which were inevitably bearing down upon Australia, they put their information in order.
2. They concerned themselves with values as they could see that these were driving change.
3. They focused on the question, "What does Australia expect of its manufacturing industry?"
4. By putting their work in a future context, common threads emerged from their diversity. In the process they changed from a committee to a community.

In their final report, they stressed the importance of people learning to adapt to the forces of change by learning to change and manage their systems to better share common aims and ideals of diverse background: "We found after a while, we were able to share a common purpose. We had field-tested among ourselves the consultative procedures which are an essential feature of the green paper."

Participation Is the Key to Progress and Adaptability The aims of the new policy were a better working economy through improving the quality of worklife, encouraging social cohesion through involving Australians in decision making, and building into institutions and processes of policy formation, "a capability to adapt to future change, whatever it may be." There should be a framework of strategy with restructuring and reduction of tariffs at the rate that revitalization and restructuring can support. In particular, they confirmed the results of the first industrial relations search by emphasizing that employees should be actively involved in making decisions that affect them with resultant dignity and satisfaction for all.

They rejected the belief that major change should be left to market forces alone: "Government should facilitate, encourage, and back with resources major structural change devised for an industry sector by participative processes within that sector."

No New Bureaucracy They recommended new participative machinery for decision making on industry policy, industry-specific councils that would form an overlapping network to generate practical and forward-looking policy. In a break with long-standing tradition, they did not recommend a super department or council, in other words, a bureaucracy.

A Big Step Backward and Steady Underlying Progress   Even though *The Jackson Report* generated huge debate and workshops were convened to put detail on the design of the industry councils, the subsequent white paper represented a massive step backward from the green paper and opened the way for the extreme economic rationalism of the 1980s. But the backward step didn't matter in the end. The prowess of the search conference had demonstrated itself to participants of the green paper search conference and since 1975, many industries have held their own search conferences to get their act together. AUSTRADE now regularly uses search conferences and other participative forms in its work to improve Australia's overseas competitiveness.

Industrial Relations Summit II: 1976

This second search focused on worker participation and industrial relations and was conducted under the same conditions as the first. *The Jackson Report* was taken as a major input and again democratic self-managing organizations were accorded primacy.

Overcoming Constraints for Participation   The managerial problems in this shift were addressed as was the need for guarantees that new participative forms could not be reversed at managerial whim. Managerial promotions should be part of a consistent approach, related to demonstrated ability to develop self management in subordinates. Legislation was seen as possibly self defeating, but collective or enterprise bargaining was endorsed with legal binding agreements for participative forms.

Work was done on their many constraints and concerns, foreshadowing some of the subsequent changes we have seen. Some examples of these concerns are:

- A massive reduction in the number of unions from 300+ craft based to about 30 industry based unions.
- More successful forms of public summit or national meetings, from bureaucratic meetings procedures to participative, as in a search conference.

There was a fear about a hierarchical super manufacturing council following the white paper and a more general concern about the influence of the public service, and particularly Treasury, in economic and social planning, or the lack of it. To overcome this potential constraint, employers participatively planned and created the Business Council of Australia to provide an appropriate environment and advice for business.

At the time of this search conference, we had a Liberal (conservative) government with a Department of Productivity which understood these matters and we expected an agreement between the government and the Australian Council of Trade Unions (ACTU) by the end of 1977. We had to wait until 1983.

Future Directions for Australia: 1980

The Future Directions conference was incidentally, the first multi-search. It had nearly 120 participants organized into four parallel search conferences of 30 each. The participants were chosen from Australia's youngest and brightest opinion leaders. Some had had contact with the events described above, some were already politicians, and others were destined to hold positions of national power and influence.

The Opposite Ends of Many Poles Had Been United   It was a dramatic and intense experience for all. "A single image etched in the mind will recall the feeling in that room. A man and a woman. A Labor Senator and a Liberal MHR, stood side by side and read in unison the third principle of their group's vision of a convivial, equitable future." Convivial equity emerged as the major scenario. It was based on four principles:

- A conserver society, democratically based, open and informed, and permeated by feminist principles, is needed to enable Australia to flourish.
- Such a society will be convivial, sharing, egalitarian, participatory, innovative, self-adjusting, consensus achieving, pluralist, and decentralized.
- A non-exploitive and internationally responsible Australia will have an Asia/Pacific orientation.
- In this convivial equity society, Australians will be more self-realizing, creative, and tolerant.

The implementation of these principles, all agreed, would require a more pluralist economic system, a more participatory politico-legal system, and more autonomous individuals. The desired result: a harmonious society, at peace.

The Industrial Relations Accord: 1983

By 1983, a national agenda had definitely emerged. It revolved around participative reconstruction and revitalization of Australian industry and democratic workplaces. It resulted in a national accord, signed between the government and the ACTU. The Summit that brought this particular agreement into being was not a search conference, but that is what the Prime Minister had in mind. He had been a member of the Jackson committee and the president of the ACTU during the subsequent formative years. And despite its less than ideal format, nothing could stop the momentum. For this idea, the time had come.

The accord created a supportive environment for microeconomic reform and workplace redesign with award restructuring. It supported payment for skills held within enterprise bargaining and more generally encouraged many of the reforms and new initiatives that had been dreamed up years before in the events described above. Its effects have not been entirely desirable nor successful in the eyes of some:

- Real wages have dropped.
- There are still pockets of resistance. Business schools are still turning out dinosaurs and the industrial courts are not well prepared to deal with the new challenges they face.

But the accord has been renegotiated almost every two years since to remain adaptive to environmental change. And as change continues, productivity increases.

The Search as Diffusion of Workplace Democratization: 1991

February 1991, saw Workplace Australia, the largest multi-search ever with over 750 participants. Its design was inspired by the Future Directions conference.

1. Its first two days were 20 search conferences in which participants planned the desirable workplace and worked on strategies to bring it into being.
2. With their frameworks clear, participants then moved into marketplace sessions where they heard case studies and swapped lessons about democratizing organizations.
   —Those who had not previously started learned from those that had.
   —Those who had experienced problems passed on their don'ts.
   —Successes were analyzed.
3. Despite its problems, there was a rash of change projects following the conference.

The conference created networks, many of them international. In Australia, new networks continued meeting back home both for diffusion and consolidation. Workplace Australia 2 was held in May, 1995.

Workplace Australia also highlighted the need for a new training course in the theory and practice of workplace democratization, through the search conference and participative design workshop. I became the bunny. The first of my new courses was held in November, 1991, and four years later, it has proven itself as a diffusion process. Several more consultants now work exclusively with these methods and the rate of effective change has increased.

COMMUNITIES CONTINUE TO COME ALIVE

The search conference continues to be a major tool in the revitalization of the Australian community. Its power has united many disparate and desperate communities and created others. It has contributed to the development of a new Australian ethos. Nowhere has it been more at home than with Australia's indigenous peoples.

WHAT HAVE WE LEARNED?

Is it really possible for any country or community to keep up or actively adapt to the change which daily assaults us? I think yes. Communities that have learned how to monitor changes in their external environment and have a democratic function and structure appropriate to the task are making it, and will continue to do so. In such communities, plans work. Their people have dignity, purpose, and meaning in life.

Can We Create or Recreate Community?

The search conference got off to its flying start in Australia in communities and it soon became clear that only communities can create community. It also became increasingly clear that the search conference definitely created communities.

Will the Search Conference Help
Us Determine Which Future We Will Live In?

There is acknowledgement that sitting down and searching for new solutions is the only answer. These agreements have emerged through the making of the change itself. In this most basic sense, the future has arrived. Given that this is the most probable future, we are walking into, those communities and organizations that can't become democratic and creative will live only to inhabit the *Jurassic Parks* of the future.

> Merrelyn Emery has been at the forefront of the development of the search conference and participative design methodology for over thirty years. Her most recent efforts have focused on the development and refinement of effective training programs for both methods. Her upcoming (co-authored) book, *Search Conferences in Action: Learning and Planning Our Way to Desirable Futures,* was published in the spring of 1996 by Jossey-Bass. This is an abridged version of an article which

appeared in the December, 1995 issue of *The Journal for Quality and Participation*.

ACKNOWLEDGEMENTS

Much of this data is taken from unpublished search conference reports. I am also indebted to Glen Watkins for up-to-date information on the regional development which led to Freemantle's defense of the America's Cup, and to Tony Ibbott for the long-term perspectives on the development of Hobart.

REFERENCES

Emery, Merrelyn. *Searching*. Amsterdam & Philadelphia: John Benjamin Publishing, 1995.

Emery, Merrelyn, and Purser, Ron. *Search Conferences in Action*. San Francisco: Jossey-Bass, 1996.

Henry, Michael, and Thompson, N. Y. (eds.) *Future Directions: 1980 Conference Report*. Melbourne: Australian Frontier, Inc. Fitzroy, 1980.

Jackson Committee. *Policies for Development of Manufacturing Industry: A Green Paper, Vol. I*. Canberra: Australian Government Publishing Service, October 1975.

Robertson, James. *The Sane Alternative*. Minneapolis, Minnesota: River Basin Publishing Company, 1978.

Sands, Angela. "The Search Conference: A Year Later." *Planning Our Town* (Emery, Merrelyn, ed.). Center for Continuing Education, Australian National University, 1974.

White, Sally. "Now to Wrap it Up . . . An Insider's View of the Conference." *The Age of Future Directions Supplement*. 18 August 1980, pp. 71-72.

Chapter 8

Requisite for Future Success: Discontinuous Improvement

Ned Hamson, AQP, and
Robert Holder, Greymatter Production

The time is 1987. Wang Laboratories, as well as Digital Equipment Corporation (DEC), are the toast of Boston, Wall Street, and the business press. A Macintosh users group meeting on the merits of PageMaker versus QuarkXPress only rates a few lines in the Boston Globe.

We live in a new era that is extremely uncomfortable. Today's much lauded firm may become the short-sighted, outdated, and outrun behemoth in a matter of months. The introduction of the Macintosh and desktop publishing in the mid to late 1980s is one of the best illustrations of how a discontinuous change and innovation can, in short order, destroy an existing marketplace and create an entirely new playing field. Massive word processing networks connected and controlled through traditional bureaucratic mechanisms were the logical extension of the typing pool and the predictable corporate markets of the early 1980s. The steel, auto, and consumer electronics industries had taken it in the neck, but the other markets and their traditional management systems seemed secure.

The idea that anyone can use a computer if they have a Macintosh or a look-alike Mac is still a bit scary to some folks. But because it matches individually controllable technology with one of the deepest and strongest trends that continues to turbulently reinvent Western society—the desire to increase the amount of control and freedom you have over your own worklife and homelife, everyday democracy—it has been wildly successful. The Mac's user friendliness trademark is now being applied to all sorts of products.

Well, you say, most have learned their lessons from that, no? Yet, today the 1995 introduction of desktop operating system and interface that emulates a 1987 Macintosh is being lauded as a great advance by the same folks who thought Wang and DEC would be the leaders for the 1990s in 1987.

So let us say this again: *This is an age of perpetual and discontinuous change and improvement—not an age of me too marketing and manufacturing!*

This revolutionary rate of change cuts across all industries:

- Twelve channels, then 90, then 150, and now 500 is only an interim estimate of what will be available via digital and satellite television. QVC and the Home Shopping Channel are killing traditional retailing and distribution of consumer goods.
- Will we, in the next year or so, be ordering our automobiles via a keypad connected to our new television/computer, specifying every detail and having it pull it up to the curb in three days?
- Saturn dealers have made a small improvement in the way we buy cars—no haggling over price—and think they have done the same thing that Toyota and Nissan did when they threw in all of the old extras in the basic auto package. Who will reinvent the way we build and buy houses? An Italian, German, Japanese, Canadian, or U.S. firm?

Perpetual and discontinuous change is turning out to not only be perpetual but the discontinuities seem to be getting greater.

TRADITIONAL WAYS OF THINKING, LEADING, AND ORGANIZING ARE OBSOLETE

Here are four reasons why:

1. Being first to market has a great impact on profitability.

Research indicates higher profitability by those first to market with products and/or services. However, focusing on single *breakthroughs* is a mistake. Firms need to support breakthroughs in manufacturing with service process improvements. A number of computer software firms have introduced great new products which have failed or may be headed for failure because they have paid no attention to improving the service processes.

Once a discontinuous improvement has been introduced, continuous improvement and the thinking on how to create your next discontinuous improvement must begin. Firms need to fuse continuous and discontinuous improvement. Casio, the consumer electronics gadget maker knows this well. So does Rubbermaid. The Rubbermaid folks know well that numerous competitors can create knock-offs of their new product in a short period of time. Their challenge and that of Casio is to constantly reinvent their product lines. The only surprising aspect of this is that surprisingly few companies have chosen to emulate the success of these two in some manner or another. Instead, they keep trying to reinvent the first plain paper copier or the new Mustang.

2. Innovation and creating new games is critical to the growth and development of human organizations.

    Americans have mastered the breakthrough process. Silicon Valley represents the breakthrough crown jewels. But we have ignored fusion innovation.

    What's fusion innovation? Fusion brings together different technologies, business functions, and management processes to create new products and services. The introduction of desktop publishing took a machine that had been used as a faster and easier-to-use typewriter and fused the jobs of writer, copyeditor, typesetter, layout artist, and paste-up technician into one person's hands. In fact, our breakthrough mastery has inhibited us from playing the new game of fusion.

3. Failure to enact discontinuous changes can cost enterprises millions, if not billions, in lost opportunity profits.

    Xerox created numerous discontinuous ideas and products without launching them. The Macintosh, personal copiers, and personal desktop laser copies are three examples. The Macintosh, an irregular computer, has set the new standard in the computer market. Developed by Xerox and discovered by Apple, it was ignored by the former because of devotion to fighting the *last war*. This was also the case with personal copiers. Xerox stayed with the past war. Canon and other Japanese firms saw a new one. This strategic blindspot has cost Xerox dearly in lost opportunity profits.

4. Management practices such as TQM, downsizing, and re-engineering may improve existing operations, short-run performance, and profits but they may not improve long-term enterprise development in a competitive and global environment.

    Unlike their American peers, Japanese managers have placed new business and product development and continuous improvement as their primary priorities while Americans focus only on quality improvement and re-engineering (reshuffling) existing structures.

DISCONTINUOUS CHANGE DEFINED

Is discontinuous change and improvement just one thing or several? It's several things. It is the reconceptualizing of a product or service in one or more of four ways:

1. It makes doing something much, much easier.
   a. It combines several tasks/functions into one operation.
   b. It enables you to do something that could not be done by an individual prior to its introduction.
2. It greatly speeds up some processes.
3. A redefinition of beauty/style/feel/sensuality that makes the product or service much more enjoyable.
4. It greatly reduces cost while not sacrificing quality.

In short, continuity with the past is broken—seemingly forever and at once:

- Federal Express reinvented small parcel delivery.
- The 1980s fax reinvented letter and memo delivery by destroying time.
- E-mail is reinventing letter and mail delivery by destroying time and space.
- Internet chat lines and the World Wide Web may well be reinventing all of the above.

If you are not familiar with the new information technologies, then think about how the VCR has changed the movie industry and what the microwave has done to traditional cooking. If we haven't given enough product examples yet, go to any store that sells recorded music and try to buy a vinyl record album. In less than two years, CDs destroyed a market that had thrived and existed for at least 80 years!

Warning! Discontinuous Change Isn't Limited to Technology and Products

Services and human systems can also experience discontinuous change and improvement. Wal-Mart hasn't created a technological breakthrough; its breakthrough was in fusing distribution, technology, and service. Ford's critical discontinuous improvement wasn't the Model T or Model A; its revisioning of organizational life and production systems was discontinuous with its time.

John Guaspari laid out the foundation for this view of discontinuous improvement in his article "So that's what we should be doing?" a few years ago. His article was on considering and charting the entire transaction with a customer and not just with the customer after the service or product is purchased. The earlier cited examples of the no-haggling Saturn buying process and Toyota's and Nissan's pricing cars with power steering and brakes and AM/FM radio tapedeck in the basic selling price illustrate how reinventing a part of the purchasing process can create a discontinuous market advantage.

The voluminous mail order catalog sales of the 1980s should have been the handwriting on the wall for department stores. What else is driving the massive concentration of the remaining national players in the department store market? It's not just bad decisions by buyers; the mode of purchasing is changing and we have excess capacity in their industry.

QVC and the Home Shopping Network are in the process of reinventing the specialty store, the department store, and the shopping mall all at once. They are redefining sales, buying, distribution, and marketing on many consumer products. A good deal of their success is based upon creating a live mail order business, combined with the speed of delivery offered by Federal Express or UPS and the atmospheres of an auction and a local shopping mall. You can watch your favorite author being interviewed, order the book, listen to people from across the country call in to say how much they like the book, and see the number of books sold in the last few minutes. If you're quick, you may be able to call in, order your book, talk briefly to the author, and have him or her personally autograph your book. Within a day or so (by the next morning if you want to pay extra) you have your personally autographed book and you never left the house!

Enough already, you say. So how can we incorporate the concepts of discontinuous improvement into our products and services? And aren't there more ways to be discontinuous? Yes, there are more ways to be discontinuous. If we'd thought of them all, we'd be sitting on a beach somewhere wondering how we would spend all our money. Seriously though (in reference to how many ways are there to be discontinuous), each market, organization, and environment consists of a somewhat unique context for discontinuity. The general concepts we have mentioned will apply in all, but only if adapted to the context of that market. To answer the first question, we will offer some images and clues for enacting and organizing discontinuous improvement.

IMAGES AND CLUES FOR ENACTING AND ORGANIZING FOR DISCONTINUOUS IMPROVEMENT

What follows is an experience in discontinuous change and improvement. Clues and images for supporting discontinuous improvement are presented. This breaks with the continuity of a conventional article in this journal. If you find yourself uncomfortable with this presentation, you may be experiencing a typical reaction to discontinuous change.

What, No Principles, Strategies, and Techniques?

Clues and images are also a discontinuous change. Most business, quality, and management works present techniques, principles, and strategies and models. To speak of discontinuous change in this fashion would be an expression of continuity which we are breaking and revisioning. It would be out of synch with the actual images of discontinuous improvement and their creators. Clues and images require the reader to experience and engage in a discontinuous improvement.

Deform Existing Images: Revision Them

Don't ask whether the enterprise is heading in the right direction but whether our images are going to create the future. Deform existing images of the enterprise, industry, products, services, organizing, and leading. Engage existing beliefs and assumptions and create new ones.

Create a Sensitive, Sensuous Enterprise

Explore existing boundaries and open them up to customers, new ideas, and fresh information. Support fusing of R&D, marketing, and manufacturing. Deploy scouting parties to get close and in touch with customers, competitors, new ideas, and fresh information. Experience people and events in a sensuous fashion and not through abstractions such as statistics, marketing reports, and consultants.

Support the Novice Effect

Recognize that professionals and experienced persons may be locked into a fixed mindset which limits their ability to perceive and/or create discontinuous improvements. Encourage people to ask:

- Why are we doing it this way?
- What is our image and metaphor?
- What other images and metaphors might be used?

Encourage people to look and be stupid, foolish, and naive about what is and what could be? Don't engage in analysis but revision to change perceptions.

Support and watching how people and customers use products—Go out and watch customers and people shopping and using products and services. (Read Yoshihara's excerpt in this book on managing innovation.) Keep in mind the cost, beauty, speed and ease of use/hassle in use concepts. How would you reinvent the kitchen, preparation of meals, use of the refrigerator? What are the most hassle producing aspects of maintaining an automobile?

A: Time pressures; refrigerators as an indistinguishable commodity; fridge magnets and messages. Make a message board built into the refrigerator to differentiate your product and please the customer.

B: Messiest and most hassle filled part of owning a car, desire to maintain a clean environment; need to save money and time. Combine the oil filter, pump and sump into a modular unit that can be easily removed, replaced and recycled. Gain an edge for your product.

Support the love and romancing of the business, products, and customer—Seek out and support people and leaders who fall in love with product and service ideas. Support romantics with stars in their ideas who seem impractical as youthful lovers but with the conviction and foresight to create revolutionary changes. Big dreams are the only ones likely to create discontinuous improvements.

Practice suicide leadership—Create a systemic process for killing off products, services, organizing and leading images, and management practices. Engage in Bohemian dialogues to support agenda-less assessments for suicide. Honor the past and recognize that rituals of passing may be required. Be aware that people may resist. This is natural. Accept their resistance rather than suppress it. Resistance made public can serve as a means to charge the innovation process with more energy.

Encourage and support creative madness—Develop a culture where *weird, unique,* and *strange* are nicknames to which people will aspire. Create the time-space for madness and provide resources for people experiencing creative madness. Recognize normality is a pathology called mediocrity. Encourage people to discover their uniqueness and express it openly.

(Who's in the picture? A young Salvador Dali, his wife/model Gala, Jung, and editor Hamson.)

Figure 8.1 Ideas and Images for Supporting and Creating Discontinuous Improvement

Unleash the Organizational Soul

Unleash the whole organization soul. Value the messy, confusing, and complex. Turn over cultural boulders to uncover values and norms which support conformity. Scout the depths and darkness for unexpressed ideas and relationships. Support reflection and imagination to deal with difficulties.

Support a Hermes Consciousness

Consciously re-vision and see the world as alive and dynamic. Look into things deeply. Encourage and reward stealing ideas from outside the enterprise from other departments. Support swift application. Support traveling and scouting. Engage people to question traditions, the established order, and be muscular about it.

Support Team and Enterprise Deepening and Rooting

Create time and space for people to gather together. Provide resources for *high touch-high tech* experiences. Provide teams with the authority to continue to work together. Deepen and create synaptic relationships between suppliers, marketing, manufacturing, and researchers. Create systems for people to develop depthful knowledge and roots.

Create a Whitewater Culture in Your Workplace

Discontinuous improvements aren't safe, they are dangerous—they destroy relationships and create mapless territories. Abandon the notion of safety, guaranteed returns, predictability, and the sure thing attitude. Forget market research and analysis. Follow T.E. Lawrence's idea that dangerous men are those who act on their dreams and appreciate the situation.

Think of Your Products and Services as Gifts for Those Who You Love

In your business, what could you make or provide that would make a loved one's life easier or more beautiful?

> "My mother-in-law has 10% vision and a close friend isn't doing well after a cataract operation. I imagine that there must be people at Apple with loved ones with similar sight problems. That's why I can't imagine why they haven't already bundled their Simple Text software (which can read text aloud), their Newton handheld computers, and optical recognition software with handheld scanning technology at a reasonable price. With an aging population staring all manufacturers in the face, the idea of providing people with failing vision an inexpensive means to read anything, anytime they want to should be appealing. But it's not on the market yet, is it."
>
> HAMSON

Think About Making Products or Services to Give Away

Ma Bell made billions by, in effect, giving your parents a telephone. They made their money by charging you for using it and making long distance calls. If we were in charge of the companies selling direct satellite television (and soon other information services), we wouldn't be charging $600 to $800 dollars for the small dish that goes on the roof. We would be nearly giving it away! If it were priced at about the same cost as the average VCR, it would take the market by storm, thus assuring that the dish and not cable will be the average home's connection to the information and entertainment highway.

If we were running Blockbuster Video stores right now, we'd make a special deal with a VCR manufacturer and sell VCRs at our stores for $49.95. Why? The videotape rental market may have a short life span with 500 channels looming on the horizon. Giving away inexpensive VCRs for a year may enable us to maximize our profits in rentals and give us the time to reinvent our business.

CLOSING THOUGHTS

We could go on and on with more clues and ideas but that would just reinforce the need for more and more examples rather than getting on with the business of creating order out of your chaos or creating chaos in your ordered marketplace with your revolutionary new products and services. The best service we can render right now is to encourage you to *JUST DO IT!*

If your colleagues and you are still not sure of your creative abilities, here is one more clue:

1. Envision, taste, smell, feel, and hear a lavish and raucous party in your office celebrating the wildly successful launch of your new product or service.
2. Backtrack or reverse engineer how that came about.

This article first appeared in the September, 1996 issue of *The Journal for Quality and Participation*.

Robert Holder is an organizational and management development consultant. His St. Louis area firm works with a variety of profit and non-profit organizations and small enterprises. He works with teams, individuals, and organizations on creativity, strategic visioning, and human systems design through one-on-one and search conference consultations. Ned Hamson's biography is at end of Chapter 1.

Chapter 9

Navigating the Emerging Decision-Making Paradigm

Steve Barber, Barber and Gonzales

I have been asked many times to describe what I do and how I help organizations learn a new, different, and better way of making decisions. But this time it started with an out-of-right-field question that really threw me for a bit.

We were sitting in a standard issue government cafeteria in the Department of Labor, taking a break from a meeting of state directors of area labor-management committees. As I was gazing into the styrofoam cup trying to figure out how anyone could do this to coffee, the guy sitting across from me says, "What's your metaphor?"

I almost spilled my coffee as I jerked my head up to look to see who had asked such a quirky, out-of-the-blue question. The guy who asked the question was Ned Hamson. I had met him briefly that morning when the meeting started. He had asked me where I was from. After I said "Sacramento, California," he simply said, "Hmm. I grew up in L.A."

For the moment, being from L.A. helped to explain the strange question. Then he asked again, "What's your metaphor? The one that explains what you were talking about this morning?" I had to stall, since I didn't have an answer as yet. I said, "Ah, what's AQP and what do you do?" As he explained AQP and his role as editor of its journal, the metaphor began to take shape in my mind's eye. Then we had a most interesting conversation and were late in getting back to the meeting.

Even though four years have passed since that conversation, the metaphor that came to me that day still describes for me what change, changing (especially how groups make decisions), and paradigms are all about.

THE WHEN-YOU-REALIZE-YOU'LL-HAVE-TO-CHANGE METAPHOR

I'm cruising down the freeway in my very comfortable and well-broken-in car. I'm going the speed limit and suddenly I'm nearly blown off the road by some guy in something that looks like it might be a car, but I can't quite tell because it went by so fast. To keep up with whatever it was, I know I'd have to replace my engine, drive train, wheels and tires, body, and the steering system. Worse yet, I realize that I will have to do it while I'm still driving what I have because I can't afford to start from scratch. Then, just ahead I see a "No speed limit" sign.

If the metaphor fits what it felt like when you or your organization realized that change was necessary and if you are the one who will have to help the organization out of being so comfortable in its old car (organization), the next question always is: Where do we start?

As my focus is both systemic and paradigmatic, I begin with the most basic, everyday act that people in all organizations do everyday: Communicate with each other and make individual and group decisions. The style I use is interactive and makes use of lots of diagrams that compare the old and current model with the emergent model—the new paradigm of decision making and communication.

So Where Do We Start?

We begin with the basics: two parties in an organization negotiating their differences over terms and conditions of employment. What are they trying to do? They're trying to reach an agreement, right? So then, let's say that reaching an agreement is a consequence of something: a meeting of minds. A meeting of minds is a consequence of something we call *understanding*. The question is then, what creates understanding?

UNDERSTANDING UNDERSTANDING

Successful problem solving, like negotiation, is essentially a consequence of the parties to an issue, understanding it well enough to have a meeting of the minds about the issue, and the solution. Understanding, coming to know or be known in the mind of another person or group, is a consequence of communication. But what is communication? What does it look like? The interesting thing about talking and listening is that it doesn't have as much to do with words, eardrums, and vocal cords! We understand each other through communication but, how do we talk and listen? Communication involves the orchestration (as an individual or as a group) of three types of behavior: words, affect, and ritual and practice.

What Is Interest-Based Decision Making?

According to *Getting to Yes* author Roger Fisher, communication is "50% talking and 50% listening, and the most important part is the listening." An interest-based approach to communication, negotiation, and problem-solving is a non-adversarial means of achieving decisions or even just being understood in a discussion or dialogue with others. It is a collection of principles and techniques familiar to anyone. These principles include concepts such as:

• Focusing on issues not personalities
• Making decisions based on an objective reason rather than power or coercion
• Accepting all motives or interests as givens, rather than evaluating those interests as right or wrong

Interest-based decision making includes recognizing that human beings are just that and as such we usually find ourselves *in relationship* to others. Because of this, the human element in any situation must be taken into account and focused on as much as the substantive element if one is to achieve a good and lasting situation rather than a win. A win often guarantees that an enemy has just been created; one who will do everything possible to insure a lose next time, or as the late Jesse Unruh would say, "Don't get mad, get even."

Although the components are familiar, to work well and serve as a tool for developing organizational effectiveness in the face of constant change, the interest approach is most successful when introduced jointly to the parties committed to using it. The introduction is through a facilitated training and practice.

Who uses this approach? It is being used in labor relations, public policy decision making, alternative dispute resolution, international relations, economic development, counseling, planning, business, government, and more. Professionals in these fields and more are discovering that the traditional approaches are no longer effective in the face of multifaceted and constant change.

Is it effective? The approach is at one and the same time, analytic and creative. Its application in public school labor relations reduced the filing of formal complaints by 70%. Its application in international relations is visible today in South Africa and the Middle East. The interest approach is fast becoming the antidote to failed or stalled initiative in quality and participatory management in business.

According to *Getting to Yes* author Roger Fisher communication is "50% talking and 50% listening, and the most important part is the listening."

Figure 9.1   50/50 Communication

Communication Through Words

Language, either verbal or written, is used to convey information about the situation at hand. When making decisions or solving problems, there appear to be three word categories:

1. Words with which we set forth the situation or issue
2. Words used in the ritual and for affect
3. Words that memorialize solution and agreement

Communication Through Affect

Affect is non-verbal posture, body language, tone of voice, facial expression, demonstration, or lack of emotion. It includes such things as volume, intensity, and timing. It has many cultural constraints and connections, and often conveys commitment, urgency, and intensity.

Ritual and Practice

Ritual and practice involves who does or says what and when. Ritual includes assumptions and principles about how success is accomplished. It's both a learned and taught collection of steps, sequences, and protocols that guides behaviors between and among the parties to the issue.

HOW WE COMMUNICATE TO SOLVE PROBLEMS

If we think about decision making as paradigm driven, two significant and identifiable models of decision making or problem solving in the workplace can be defined: conventional communication and an emerging paradigm of communication for decision making.

The conventional communications paradigm...
Words:
° About issues: distributive
° In ritual: constrained
Affect:
° Is confrontational
° Is adversarial
Ritual:
° Is positional

The emerging communications program...
Words:
° About issues: integrative and interconnected
° In ritual they are creative and expansive
° About issues are restrictive
Affect:
° Cooperative
° Collaborative
Ritual:
° Principled

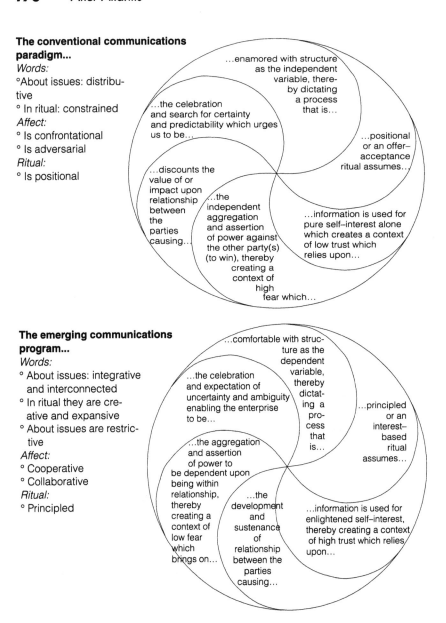

Figure 9.2 The Conventional vs. the Emerging Communications Paradigm

The Conventional Communications Paradigm

This has been the predominate paradigm used for the better part of this millennium. In Western Civilization at least, this model represents our way of escaping from the making of decisions by the assertion of raw, physical power.

The use of raw power has been diffused and/or reduced by the concept of rights and the offer/counteroffer, accept/reject method of negotiations. In the workplace, we've been practicing a version of the rights concept and the conventional communications model for about 150 years. The tug of war in the workplace or elsewhere has focused on determining where one party's rights end and another's begin. This model reflects our (now outmoded) Newtonian understanding of how the universe works—for each action, there is an equal and opposite reaction.

The Emerging Communications Paradigm

Since the rights won through confrontation or assertion concept became entrenched in law or logic, our understanding of the world has grown much more complex. We are now realizing that the conventional decision-making model is not serving us well. And we have realized that there is a need for something other than offer/counteroffer, have or have not, win or lose.

The emerging model reflects our current understanding that the universe may be understood through quantum, field, chaos, and Newtonian theories all at the same time.

What's our communication about? Most often, our communication concerns a situation, issue, dispute, problem, or an opportunity. I personally dislike the word problem and like to use opportunity instead. The negative qualities associated with it (problem child, problem worker, he/she is problematic) carry biases that preclude some choices and/or data from being considered. Semantics aside, when we communicate to reconcile different views of a situation, needs, and/or desires, it's also to settle differences over how the situation is to be resolved.

My colleague, Ian Walke, introduced me to a convenient way of entering into an analysis of any situation. He calls it CPR! I call it "Ian's triage." Any opportunity or situation can be thought of as having three fundamental components: content, process, and relationship. Each of these in turn can be further analyzed. When all these elements are understood, diagnosis, prescription, and practice are possible. A closer look at the content aspect is presented in Figure 9.4.

The Process Aspect of Decision Making

The process or ritual aspect of decision making may also be presented as alternative conventional and emerging paradigms.

The process and logistics of each offers the most visible and recognizable contrast between the two paradigms. In the conventional approach, people face off against each other as they would before the puck is dropped (ice hockey), the ball is thrown up (basketball), or the ball dropped (rugby) to begin the game.

Any opportunity or situation is suscep-
tible to analysis (taking it apart or dis-
aggregating it) as to these three
fundamental components: content,
process, and relationship. Each of
these components, in turn, is suscepti-
ble to further scrutiny. Once the elements of each component are
understood, diagnosis, prescription,
and practice are possible.

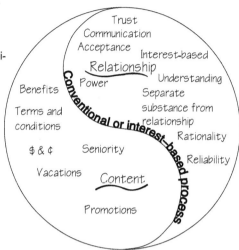

Figure 9.3   Ian's Triage for Understanding Issues and Situations

The Relationship Aspect of Decision Making

Drawing from Fisher and Brown's *Getting Together*, me and my colleague's use of the interest-based approach in many different organizations, I have found that there are eight elements to effective relationships.

When these principles are compared with the conventional model, you
begin to see why the offer-acceptance model is divisive and non-functional as
a workplace (community) building tool. A quick look at the process figure
(see Figure 9.5) demonstrates how the conventional model discounts the
importance of relationship as a variable in problem solving/decision making.

PULLING THE INTEREST-BASED PROCESS TOGETHER

To bring the principles of an interest approach to life, a dynamic sequence
of steps, techniques, and assumptions is recommended.

Those who are familiar with the brainstorming and consensus decision
making approaches should find these principles quite familiar, and should be
able to see why their use in other types of decision making will be beneficial:

- Focus on issues, not personalities.
- Describe, don't accuse.
- Tell the truth.

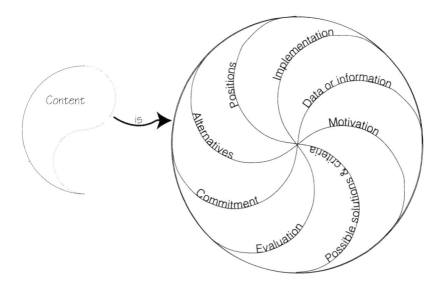

Think of yourself as the lens of a camera. What is seen when the shutter is opened and the snapshot taken are these:

Data or information .... Telling the story with perspectives too

Motive, need, interests .... Heritage, culture, Maslow, history

Positions .... The solution to which one party is committed

Possible solutions & criteria .... Multiple other prospects for solving but require agreement

Evaluative behavior .... Comparing solutions to motives and measures

Decision/commitment .... Saying "yes" or saying "no"

Alternatives .... What can be done without anyone's agreement or if can't get agreement

Implementation behavior .... Putting the solution into action

Figure 9.4   The Content Aspect of Ian's Triage

- Defer evaluation.
- Defer commitment.
- Focus on interests, not positions.
- Don't judge interests.
- Attempt to meet both separate and mutual interests.
- Develop legitimacy.
- Use consensus.
- Be systematic and celebrate learning.

The essential approach is to engage in a sequential yet dynamic application of elements and techniques to the problem (opportunity).

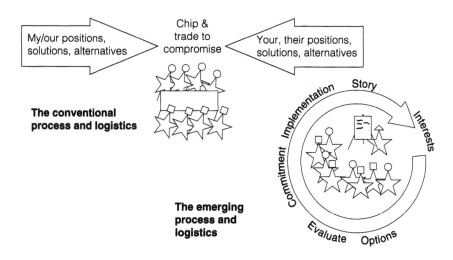

The process and logistics of each aspect offers the most visible and recognizable contrast between the two paradigms. In the conventional approach, people face off against each other as they would before the puck is dropped (ice hockey), the ball is thrown up (basketball), or the ball dropped (rugby) to begin the game.

Figure 9.5 The Process Aspect of Ian's Triage

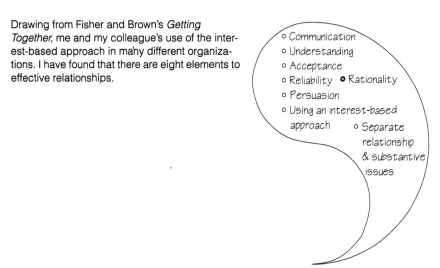

Figure 9.6 The Relationship Aspect of Decision Making

Problem issues are explained in detail and analyzed.

Interests: Discuss, answer questions about why we're here, and motivate to solve the issue.

Clarify and detail options: Establish criteria—standards for measurements are objectively agreed to by parties.

Evaluation/analysis: Comparing options to interests & criteria stimulates improvement in plan.

Consensus/commitment: Members can live with options for now and will work to achieve its success.

Implementation: What, who, when, work: Detailed procedures are outlined and responsibilities assigned.

The dynamic aspect of the approach comes into play when elements previously discussed or agreed upon reemerge. At that point, participants return to the previous step and begin the process *again* at that step.

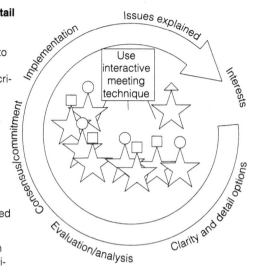

Figure 9.7   The Interest-Based Problem Solving Elements in Sequence

All of This Occurs in a Larger Setting

The larger context of practicing these principles and tools is where we discover another, fundamental principle of an interest approach to problem solving: finding, understanding, and evaluating each party's unattractive unilateral alternatives.

Knowing the alternative and the probable reaction by the other parties to its use serves as a powerful measuring device for agreement or solution which emerges from an interest approach.

HOW TO IMPLEMENT AN INTEREST-BASED PROCESS

The choice to launch a change in process and culture such as this is dramatic and significant. It involves unlearning old and ingrained habits and learning and practicing of new habits. It is very much like the struggle to recover from an addiction to accumulating and asserting power—I call those who chose to follow the new paradigm *recovering authoritarians*.

The larger context of practicing these principles and tools is where we discover another fundamental principle of an interest approach to problem solving: finding, understanding, and evaluating each party's unattractive unilateral alternatives.

An alternative in this context is something which one party can do without the agreement of the other or what any party can do if agreement cannot be reached.

The alternatives must be evaluated for their impact if actually acted out.

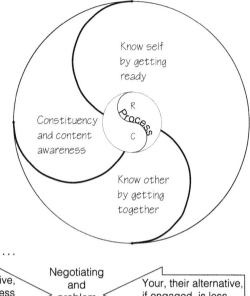

The Alternative . . .

Figure 9.8   The Larger Context of the Overall Process

Getting Started

Getting started involves joint exploration of the concept such as a joint delegation attending a conference and/or an orientation given to a joint audience (on your site) by an experienced, interest-based facilitator or practitioner. Next, an introductory training of appropriate length (3 or 5 days) is necessary. This training should be reinforced with follow-up facilitation. The need for training to be joint cannot be emphasized enough. Even with the training, practice in the principles is obligatory if you want to avoid backsliding into the traditional paradigm again. Once engaged in the interest approach, be advised that for a long time to come, you must think of yourselves as recovering authoritarians. Patience, forthrightness in reminding each other of backsliding symptoms, and determination to stay the course may sound like old needlepoint homilies, but they are necessary to your success nonetheless.

FINAL THOUGHTS

The emerging paradigm for successful decision making is not someone's grand experiment, nor is it a plug-in approach. Many organizations are using it and finding that they can rebuild their vehicle while staying on the road. They have found that with this process they can not only catch up with those already using it but they can keep pace (or even pass the folks driving the old model of the new paradigm) as the paradigm evolves into an even more flexible and effective vehicle for change.

Adjusting to the ever-changing demands of the marketplace just cannot be done in the boardroom, the R&D lab, or by purchasing new technology anymore. It takes making best use of the decision-making capabilities of everyone in the enterprise. Think of it this way: if change is a huge powerful (and fast) bulldozer, instead of a fast car—whose help won't you need to be sure your enterprise doesn't become part of the road?

> Steve Barber has spent the better part of the past decade (12,000+ hours) introducing union and management groups to non-adversarial means of labor relations and negotiation. Barber, a native of Taft, California, served a variety of posts (including that of deputy director) during 15 years of service in California's Public Employment Relations Board. Barber's groundbreaking work at PERB led to the creation of the California Foundation for the Improvement of Employer-Employee Relations (CFIER).

REFERENCES

This short bibliography will provide you with some windows into the emerging paradigm. Each of these books in turn contains substantial references for further reading and inquiry.

1. Barber, Stephen. "Letting genies out of bottles." *The Journal for Quality and Participation,* January/February, 1993.

2. Barber, Stephen, "What do you mean . . . I might be illegitimate?" *The Journal for Quality and Participation,* January/February 1994.

3. Fisher, Roger, and Brown, Scott, *Getting Together: Building Relationships As We Negotiate,* New York: Penguin Books, 1988.

4. Fisher, Roger, and Ury, William, *Getting To Yes: Negotiating Agreement Without Giving In,* New York: Penguin Books, 1983. This is an abridged version of an article which appeared in the March, 1995 issue of *The Journal for Quality and Participation.*

For Product Safety Concerns and Information please contact our EU
representative GPSR@taylorandfrancis.com Taylor & Francis Verlag GmbH,
Kaufingerstraße 24, 80331 München, Germany

Batch number: 08158437

Printed by Printforce, the Netherlands